EXTRAORDINARY RECIPES FROM

PROVIDENCE & RHODE ISLAND CHEF'S TABLE

LINDA BEAULIEU

Photography by Al Weems

THE OCEAN STATE

LYONS PRESS

Guilford, Connecticut

An imprint of Globe Pequot Press

Restaurants and chefs often come and go, and menus are ever changing.
We recommend you call ahead to obtain current information before visiting any
of the establishments in this book.

Lyons Press is an imprint of Globe Pequot Press.

All photography by Al Weems

Editor: Amy Lyons
Project Editors: Lynn Zelem and Lauren Brancato
Text Design: Libby Kingsbury
Layout Artist: Nancy Freeborn

Library of Congress Cataloging-in-Publication Data is available on file.

ISBN 978-0-7627-9662-5

Printed in the United States of America

10 9 8 7 6 5 4 3 2 1

To all the great chefs of
Rhode Island, with much
appreciation and admiration.

CONTENTS

RECIPES BY COURSE

SIDE DISHES

DESSERTS

COCKTAIL

Acknowledgments

To write this book I went on a four-month journey that took me into more than fifty restaurant kitchens, from Providence outward to Newport, South County, and the suburbs. As always, it was a real treat to be inside those kitchens with our finest chefs and restaurant owners, learning their latest thoughts on food.

Accompanying me on this amazing experience was photographer extraordinaire Al Weems. I've known Al for years and worked with him a bit in the past, but our four months on the road showed me firsthand how truly talented this man is (and how easy he is to get along with). After a full day in Newport or an afternoon in Narragansett, Al would e-mail me samples of his day's work. He never disappointed me. Time and time again I found his food photos to be not just beautiful, but interesting as well. Now that our journey has ended, I miss riding shotgun in Al's bright red Toyota, affectionately known as "the clown car."

I also want to thank my editor, Amy Lyons, Editorial Director, Travel and Regional Cooking, Globe Pequot Press, for the opportunity to work on this wonderful project. This is the book I've always wanted to write, and I so appreciate the chance to do so. And thank you, Project Editors Lynn Zelem and Lauren Brancato, for guiding me through the final editing process.

Every writer needs an editor. I'm especially fortunate in that area for I am married to a now-retired journalist. Brian Beaulieu has been my at-home editor for more than thirty years. He always helps me perfect my writing before I send it off for publication.

I especially want to thank all the chefs and restaurant owners who participated in this book project. More than fifty chefs are profiled in this book from restaurants throughout the state. They submitted more than 150 recipes, some relatively easy and some definitely for the accomplished home cook. These chefs welcomed us warmly into their kitchens and accommodated our every need during their photo sessions.

And to the readers, if your favorite chef and restaurant isn't in this book, please know that we tried . . . and tried. More than one hundred restaurants were invited to be in *Providence & Rhode Island Chef's Table,* and we suspect that their invitations are probably still on their desks, somewhere under a pile of unopened mail. We understand—chefs are hardworking men and women, incredibly busy, in their kitchens far more than forty hours a week. So please know that we recognize their talent and accomplishments, and we certainly would have liked all of them to be in this book. For her special efforts in this area, I would like to thank my good friend Deborah Moxham, who persuaded several key chefs to open their mail and accept my invitation to be in *Providence & Rhode Island Chef's Table.*

Introduction

Here it is—the book I've been wanting to write for years. In my three decades as a food writer, I like to think I've grown and gotten better at what I love to do, just as the Rhode Island restaurant scene has improved *immensely,* from Providence to Newport and beyond. It all started in Providence in the 1970s, when there were very few great restaurants in the state.

Rue de l'Espoir and Pot au Feu were the early pioneers, serving French cuisine and bistro fare. Julia Child often said her favorite Providence restaurant was Pot au Feu. Al Forno and New Rivers opened in 1980, both garnering national acclaim for their Modern Italian cuisine and New American cuisine, respectively. Not surprisingly, these four wonderful restaurants are still in business today. They may have reinvented themselves every now and then, but their continued success is a testament to their culinary vision. It was those venerable restaurants and chefs that brought media attention to little Rhode Island. So many chefs and restaurateurs deserve to be mentioned: Deb Norman from Rue de l'Espoir, Bob Burke from Pot au Feu, George Germon and Johanne Killeen from Al Forno, Bruce Tillinghast from New Rivers, John Elkhay now from Chow Fun Food Group, Casey Riley now from Newport Restaurant Group, Ralph Conte now from Plum Point Bistro, and Jaime d'Oliveira, now a restaurant consultant. If Rhode Island had a foodie hall of fame, these well-established culinary stars would all deserve a place there.

Standing on their shoulders is a whole new generation of young chefs, members of the new progressive food movement—several whose forearms are tattooed works of art, symbolic of their renegade spirit. They are equally passionate about their food and where it comes from—Nick Rabar from Avenue N, Brian Kingsford from Bacaro, Matt Gennuso from Chez Pascal, Nemo Bolin from Cook & Brown, Matt Jennings from Farmstead, Matt Varga from Gracie's, Beau Vestal from New Rivers, Derek Wagner from Nicks on Broadway, Champe Speidel from Persimmon, Jake Rojas from Tallulah on Thames, and so many more. They have all formed close ties to local farmers and fishermen to ensure the freshest possible ingredients are delivered regularly to their kitchens.

At the center of this exciting food scene is Providence. The state of Rhode Island is so small, it's more like a city-state with just about everything within easy driving distance. When Chef Rich Silvia leaves his White Horse Tavern in Newport late at night, he often heads into Providence for a midnight nosh at Nicks on Broadway before heading home to Warwick. A growing number of chefs are making their mark initially in Providence and then moving out to the not-so-distant suburbs, folks such as Kevin Millonzi at Millonzi's Bar & Grille in West Warwick and Angie Armenise at Blackie's Bulldog Tavern in Smithfield. Rhode Island really is like one big city, much like Los Angeles, where you can drive thirty minutes in any direction and find restaurants worthy of your time and money.

During the past thirty years, I've written about all these chefs for local publications and in my previous books. It began with *Divine Providence: An Insider's Guide to*

Providence's Best Restaurants, and then *The Grapevine Guide to Rhode Island's Best Restaurants,* which I co-wrote with Deborah Moxham. My *Providence and Rhode Island Cookbook* is a collection of recipes unique to the region. Then came this opportunity to write *Providence & Rhode Island Chef's Table,* a hardcover book profiling the very best chefs of Rhode Island with color photography—the book I'd been wanting to write for years.

I was born in Rhode Island and grew up right over the state line in Massachusetts. I have wonderful childhood memories, mostly dealing with food. We had a milkman who brought us fresh milk in glass bottles from Wild Acres Dairy, and a baker who stopped in weekly with freshly made breads in the back of his station wagon. My father would take me blueberry picking in the summer, and we would drive out to buy fresh corn on the cob at local farms every weekend. Swordfish was incredibly inexpensive back then, and we had it almost every Friday night. We spent our Sundays on the Rhode Island seacoast—visiting relatives on primitive Hog Island where we dug for clams, frolicking on the beach in Narragansett, or having a shore dinner at legendary Rocky Point, now gone. My family loved being in the Ocean State. Seafood was very important to my parents, and they always sought out the best restaurants serving steamed clams and clam cakes—nothing fancy, just really good, really fresh food. It was a way of life that reminds me of today's chefs who are preparing food that is as locally sourced as possible.

Thanks to the media, the rest of the world is learning about Providence, Rhode Island, and its appeal to foodies:

- *Saveur* magazine included Providence among the best small cities for restaurants and dining in the world as part of its 2013 Culinary Travel Awards. According to *Saveur,* small cities are those with a population under 800,000. Providence was one of a handful of American cities to make the notable list, which included Las Vegas, Nevada, and Miami, Florida. Internationally, the prestigious list included Florence, Italy, and Edinburgh, Scotland.

- After visiting Providence in 2013, Andrew Zimmern from the Travel Channel said: "There are chefs here who are absolutely, doggedly committed to the ingredients coming out of the farms and the oceans. It's a brilliant city to be eating through right now."

- If you do an Internet search for "best food city," Providence pops up, beating out the legendary food meccas of Chicago, Manhattan, New Orleans, and San Francisco. In 2013, *Travel + Leisure* magazine declared Providence to be "the #1 Food City" in the United States after conducting a nationwide poll. *Travel + Leisure* readers also voted Providence the number-one city for burgers and for pizza.

It's nice to be so richly recognized, but we Rhode Islanders knew it all along. The Ocean State's food tradition endures, and it will continue, for it is in very capable hands.

PROVIDENCE

AL FORNO

577 SOUTH MAIN STREET
PROVIDENCE, RI 02903
(401) 273-9760
ALFORNO.COM
EXECUTIVE CHEF DAVID REYNOSO
OWNERS GEORGE GERMON AND JOHANNE KILLEEN

Al Forno just might be the most famous restaurant in Rhode Island. Since it opened in 1980, it has been receiving well-deserved publicity on a national level. The awards—including being named the best casual restaurant in the world—are too numerous to mention.

Al Forno is the creation of George Germon and Johanne Killeen, a husband-and-wife team who met at the Rhode Island School of Design. Their training in the fine arts is visible in every one of their creations, from their famous grilled pizza to their Dirty Steak with Hot Fanny Sauce. The original Al Forno was a tiny space at the foot of College Hill, where New Rivers is located today. With almost instant success, it quickly became necessary for Al Forno to move to its current location on the Providence waterfront.

Located in a charming old brick building, Al Forno is entered through an arched doorway and an alfresco dining area, simply beautiful spring through fall. On a warm

summer night, it's where you want to be for a perfect dining experience. Inside, there are two floors of dining possibilities with separate kitchens on both levels. The rustic yet sophisticated interior has evolved over the years and continues to do so on a seasonal basis. White marble floor tiles and charcoal gray walls frame the long, narrow dining space, accented with varying shades of green and just a bit of soft purple trim. Every table is set perfectly with white linens. A popular area especially in winter is the romantic bar with its huge fireplace. The finishing touches change with the seasons—an abundance of flowers and greenery in the summer, bright yellow corncobs still in their husks and orange pumpkins of all sizes in the fall.

This is a restaurant known for its regional Italian cuisine. The menu also recognizes the importance of local ingredients under the supervision of Executive Chef David Reynoso, who has been with Germon and Killeen for almost two decades. Al Forno is especially known for its wood-grilled dishes, garlic mashed potatoes, and freshly made desserts including my favorite, the Grand Cookie Finale for two or more with its warm chocolate-ricotta fritters and candied citrus peel.

Two delicious cookbooks featuring Al Forno's recipes have been published to date. Just about every celebrity who comes to Providence dines at Al Forno, it is that well known.

Lobster Risotto

(SERVES 8 AS AN APPETIZER)

Chef Reynoso's note: This dish was created especially for President Obama on one of his trips to Rhode Island. Be sure to use a wooden spoon rather than metal to stir the rice. Metal spoons conduct heat and get too hot to handle without a potholder.

For the risotto:

4 live lobsters, 1½ pounds each
2 quarts chicken stock, preferably homemade
1½ cups lobster stock (preferably homemade, recipe follows)
2 tablespoons extra-virgin olive oil
4 tablespoons unsalted butter, at room temperature, divided

2 large shallots, peeled and finely diced
1 teaspoon sea salt
4 ounces fresh chanterelle mushrooms, cleaned, trimmed, and sliced
1½ cups carnaroli rice
2 teaspoons chopped chives

For the lobster stock:

4 tablespoons extra-virgin olive oil

Reserved lobster shells from 4 lobsters

2 medium onions, root ends removed, peeled, and
coarsely chopped

2–3 carrots, peeled and coarsely chopped

2 garlic cloves, peeled and chopped

1 fennel bulb, washed and coarsely chopped

2 celery stalks, washed and coarsely chopped

1 leek, trimmed, carefully washed to remove any
sand, and coarsely chopped

1 cup dry white wine

2 cups canned whole tomatoes, chopped

Bouquet garni (bay leaf, peppercorns, and thyme
wrapped in cheesecloth)

Salt, to taste

8 tablespoons (1 stick) unsalted butter

To make the risotto: Plunge the lobsters in lightly salted boiling water and cook for 6 minutes. Transfer the lobsters to an ice bath to chill. Drain well and place the lobsters on a cutting board.

Snap off the claws and knuckles. Separate the tails from the bodies. Split the tails in half lengthwise. Remove the tail meat, reserving the shells. Cut the tail meat into four bite-size pieces each and set aside. Crack open the knuckles and claws, reserving the shells. Remove the meat and set aside with the tail meat. Divide all the lobster meat into eight equal piles or portions on a baking sheet. Cover with foil and refrigerate.

Rinse the lobster head and body in cold water. Carefully remove the gritty tomalley sac and discard. Cover and refrigerate all the shells from the lobsters if you are making lobster stock.

Bring the chicken stock to a boil in a stockpot. Reduce the heat to maintain a gentle simmer. In a saucepan, bring the lobster stock to a boil,

reduce the heat to the lowest setting, cover with the lid slightly ajar, and keep warm.

Preheat the oven to 350°F.

In a heavy-bottomed saucepan, heat the olive oil with 2 tablespoons of the butter. Add the shallots and salt, and sauté over moderately high heat, stirring often, until the shallots are translucent and cooked through, about 10 minutes. Add the mushrooms and sauté until the liquid from the mushrooms has evaporated. Add the rice and stir, making sure each individual grain of rice is coated with oil. Sauté, stirring constantly, for a few minutes to toast the rice. It will change from translucent to slightly opaque.

Add about ½ cup of the simmering chicken stock to the rice, stirring constantly. The stock will be absorbed quickly. Add another ½ cup of chicken stock, stirring constantly. Continue to add stock, ½ cup at a time, stirring frequently, as the chicken stock is absorbed into the rice but before it evaporates completely. The rice should never look dry. Regulate the heat so the stock boils rapidly. The rice should be cooked al dente—or firm to the tooth—in 15–18 minutes. Taste after 13 minutes and every minute thereafter, to be sure not to overcook, until the risotto is cooked al dente and a bit runny. If it seems too stiff or dry, add a few tablespoons of stock (keep in mind you may not need all the chicken stock). Stir in the remaining butter.

Approximately 10–12 minutes before the risotto is finished, heat the lobster meat, covered, in the oven. Check after 7 minutes. The lobster should be heated through but not overcooked.

Divide the risotto among eight heated rimmed soup bowls, and arrange a portion of lobster on top of each. Spoon the lobster stock over and around each portion. Garnish with chives and serve immediately.

To make the lobster stock: Heat the olive oil in a stockpot. Add the lobster shells and brown on all sides, about 10–15 minutes. Add all the vegetables except the canned tomatoes, and simmer the mixture gently for 10 minutes. Add the white wine and cook over high heat until all the wine has evaporated. Add the tomatoes and simmer for 10 minutes.

Pour in 1 quart of boiling water along with the bouquet garni. Bring to a boil, lower the heat, and simmer gently for 1 hour.

Strain the stock through a fine strainer into a clean pan. Cook the stock until about 1½ cups remain. Taste and add salt if you like. Whisk the butter into the stock just before serving.

Angelo's Civita Farnese

141 Atwells Avenue
Providence, RI 02903
(401) 621-8171
ANGELOSRI.COM
Owner Bob Antignano

This is as old school as it can get. Angelo's Civita Farnese, named after a tiny town twelve miles west of Rome, opened its doors in 1924, welcoming the workingman and his family. The owner was Angelo Mastrodicasa, who envisioned a no-frills restaurant serving simple Italian food that was hearty and substantial and inexpensive. The food was served on white glass–topped communal tables, and it still is. Customers continue to dine at those tables, but now they sit elbow to elbow with local politicians, businessmen, celebrities, and college students who have discovered Angelo's delicious food and reasonable prices.

In 1988, the business was handed over to a nephew, Bob Antignano, who still runs the restaurant. Angelo's underwent a renovation in 2006. The popular restaurant was modernized, but it still retains the Old World character that customers love so much. The new Angelo's is twice as big with wood wainscoting, dark booths, and a black-and-white checkerboard floor. Old photos hang on the light-colored walls, and fresh herbs grow in indoor window boxes. Those original communal tables are still there, as is an elevated model railroad which, for a quarter, makes its way around the entire dining room, much to the delight of children. The proceeds benefit children's charities in Rhode Island.

But the food is the thing, to paraphrase Shakespeare, at Angelo's. The southern Italian food on the menu is what really draws people back again and again to this Federal Hill restaurant. The menu changes with the seasons, but there are certain dishes that are always available, such as the simple pastine soup, traditional fried calamari and smelts, snail salad, tripe, eggplant parmesan, roasted chicken, and the award-winning veal and peppers.

When it comes to pasta, you have a choice of spaghetti, penne, cavatelli, whole wheat, and homemade pasta, plus lasagna and ravioli. Many Italian families refer to their pasta sauce as "gravy," which is made fresh daily at Angelo's. There are three gravies on the menu: the original house sauce, marinara, and a veggie sauce. Almost the entire menu is priced under $15, with most dishes well below that amount. Make sure you try the limoncello cake for dessert.

Lunch is always a busy time at Angelo's. On any given day the crowd consists of executives in suits, young couples, the elderly, and three generations of family at a single table. Regular customers know it's best to park in the rear of the restaurant, where free valet parking is available.

SAUSAGE SPECIAL

SAUSAGE, POTATOES, PEPPERS & ONIONS

(SERVES 4)

2 pounds sweet Italian sausage, cut into 3-inch pieces

1 cup blended vegetable and olive oil, divided

2 teaspoons black pepper, more or less to taste, divided

2 teaspoons granulated garlic, more or less to taste, divided

3 large boiling potatoes, peeled and cut lengthwise into wedges

2 large green bell peppers, cored and cut into wide strips

1 large red bell pepper, cored and cut into wide strips

2 medium white onions, skin removed and cut into chunks

Preheat oven to 375°F. Place a rack in the center of the oven.

Place the sausage in a large baking pan. Drizzle with ¼ cup of the oil, 2 teaspoons of black pepper, and 2 teaspoons of granulated garlic. Mix well and bake for 20 minutes. Remove the pan from the oven, mix well, and continue baking for 10 more minutes.

Remove the pan from the oven. Add the potato wedges, 2 teaspoons of black pepper, and 2 teaspoons of granulated garlic. Drizzle with ¼ cup of oil. Mix well and bake for 20 minutes. Remove the pan from the oven, mix well, and continue baking for 10 more minutes.

Remove the pan from the oven. Add the peppers, onions, and remaining black pepper and garlic. Drizzle with the remaining oil, mix well, and bake for 10–15 minutes.

Remove the pan from the oven. Mix well, and bake for an additional 10–15 minutes. Serve immediately.

Spring Chicken

BAKED CHICKEN CUTLET WITH MIXED GREENS

(SERVES 4)

For the chicken:

1¼ pounds thinly sliced boneless chicken cutlets
1 cup flour
2 large eggs
1 cup water
1 teaspoon salt
1 teaspoon ground black pepper
1 teaspoon garlic powder
1 cup Italian bread crumbs

For the mixed greens:

4 cups mixed spring greens
1 cup diced tomatoes
4–6 ounces bottled balsamic vinaigrette dressing

To make the chicken: Preheat oven to 375°F. Place a rack in the center of the oven.

Place the sliced boneless chicken cutlets between two pieces of plastic wrap. Gently pound the slices to about ½ inch thick.

Place the flour in a shallow bowl or plate.

In a shallow bowl, beat the eggs, water, salt, pepper, and garlic powder until well blended.

Spread the bread crumbs on a piece of wax paper or a baking sheet.

Cover both sides of each pounded cutlet in the flour, and then place the cutlets in the egg mixture. Remove the cutlets from the egg mixture, and place them in the bread crumbs. Completely cover both sides of each cutlet with bread crumbs.

Place the cutlets on a baking sheet, and put the baking sheet in the preheated oven. Bake for 8 minutes, flip the cutlets over, and continue to bake for 8 more minutes. While the cutlets are baking, assemble the mixed greens.

To prepare the mixed greens: In a large bowl, combine the mixed spring greens with the diced tomatoes and half of the balsamic vinaigrette dressing. Set the bowl aside in the refrigerator.

To serve: When the cutlets are finished baking, move them to a serving platter. Drizzle the cutlets with the remaining dressing and top with the mixed greens. Serve immediately.

Bacaro

262 South Water Street
Providence, RI 02903
(401) 751-3700
BACARORESTAURANT.NET
Executive Chef Brian Kingsford

Housed in a red brick building from the 1800s, Bacaro has a handsome twelve-seat bar framed by huge rough-hewn wood beams. Fresh flowers adorn every table, formally set with crisp white linens. A color scheme of soft greens and golds is seen throughout the sophisticated Italian restaurant. In warm weather, the wrought-iron patio is in much demand, centered by a soothing water fountain and surrounded with bright yellow hibiscus and cascading purple and white flowers. Old-fashioned street lamps light the area at night.

With its split concept, Bacaro is many things to different people. The street level is an *enoteca, salumeria,* and *cicchetteria,* patterned after the *bacari* of Venice. Translated, Bacaro is a wine bar, where friends gather for a quick bite of cured meats and cheeses, all on display in the *salumeria* where prosciutto and fontina are hand cut to order on a bright red slicing machine imported from Italy. Guests are handed long lists of what's available, including olives from Puglia and *spuntini* (snacks), all served with fresh bread and Tuscan olive oil. The "snacks" are the Italian version of tapas, including lightly fried *burrata* with San Marzano tomatoes, grilled purses of mortadella stuffed with Taleggio cheese, crostini with olive tapenade, and marinated artichokes with fresh herbs.

Those longing for full dinners are seated on the second floor, which offers dramatic views of the Providence River and downtown Providence as well as a look inside the open kitchen. The young chefs explore the wonderful food of Italy, under the watchful eye of the executive chef and owner of Bacaro, Brian Kingsford. His partner, Jennifer Matta, skillfully oversees the front of the house, making sure every guest is greeted warmly.

The secret to their success is that the ever-changing menu always offers what their guests feel like eating. "Our dishes speak to the season," said Chef Kingsford. "Summer is our favorite time of year as the variety of produce at Confreda Farm keeps us constantly creating in the kitchen." On any given morning in the summer and early fall, Kingsford and Matta can be found picking their own vegetables in the fields of Confreda Farm. When the tomatoes are at their ripest and the basil is perfectly sweet, it's time for Bacaro's Spaghetti Caprese to hit the menu.

"This simple pasta is based on a few perfect ingredients, making it an unforgettable dish," Chef Kingsford said. "But it's only as good as the ingredients used to make it. Always take the time to find the freshest and highest quality tomatoes and basil."

Spaghetti Caprese
with Sweet Summer Tomatoes & Basil

(SERVES 6)

For the spaghetti:

½ cup kosher salt

1½ pounds high-quality dried spaghetti, such as
Garofolo or Rustichella d'Abruzzo

5 ripe tomatoes, cut into ¼-inch slices

4 fresh mozzarella balls (buffalo or cow's milk),
cut into ¼-inch slices

1 cup pesto (recipe follows)

½ cup pasta water

Estate-grown and estate-bottled extra-virgin olive oil,
such as Zisola or Olio Verde from Sicily

Maldon flaked sea salt

Parmigiano-Reggiano, for grating as garnish

For the pesto: (Makes 2 cups)

1 pint firmly packed basil leaves

1 garlic clove, crushed

½ cup pignoli (pine nuts)

⅔ cup extra-virgin olive oil

Kosher salt, to taste

To make the spaghetti: Bring 8 quarts of water to a boil in a large pot. When it comes to a boil, generously salt the water with kosher salt. Drop the pasta into the boiling water and cook until al dente, about 10–15 minutes depending on the brand of pasta used. Be sure to stir the pasta often during the cooking time to keep it from sticking together.

While the pasta is cooking, layer the slices of tomato and mozzarella around the outer rim of a large platter, leaving enough room in the center for the cooked pasta.

Place the pesto in a bowl large enough for tossing the pasta.

When the pasta is al dente, strain it, but reserve about ½ cup of the pasta water for loosening up the sauce, if needed. Place the cooked pasta in the bowl with the pesto, and toss to coat evenly. Add the pasta water, if needed, a little bit at a time until the desired consistency is reached.

Drizzle the extra-virgin olive oil over the tomatoes and mozzarella slices, and sprinkle with the Maldon sea salt. Place the pasta in the center of the platter. Garnish generously with freshly grated Parmigiano-Reggiano and serve.

To make the pesto: Place the basil, garlic, and pignoli into the bowl of a food processor. Pulse until well combined. With the food processor running, slowly drizzle in the olive oil until well combined. Season to taste with salt.

THE CAFE AT EASY ENTERTAINING

166 VALLEY STREET
PROVIDENCE, RI 02909
(401) 437-6090
EASYENTERTAININGRI.COM
EXECUTIVE CHEF KAITLYN ROBERTS

What's not to like about The Cafe at Easy Entertaining, a converted factory loft where you can get a delightful breakfast and a creative lunch, or you can plan your next catered event. The Cafe is an offshoot of Easy Entertaining, a catering company owned and operated by Chef Kaitlyn Roberts, who went to culinary school in Florence, Italy.

You'll be greeted warmly as you enter The Cafe, which consists of a very large room with oversize windows and lots of interesting decor, from elephant-based lamps to delicate chandeliers—simply charming. Whether the sun is pouring in on a beautiful spring day or a wintry rain is pelting those windows, you'll find a farm-to-fork menu filled with seasonal offerings. Most of the ingredients come from local purveyors and farms.

In the summer, the signature BLT combines applewood-smoked bacon, mixed greens, sliced tomatoes, and roasted garlic aioli on your choice of brioche or whole-grain and flax bread. The New England lobster roll sports a quarter pound of freshly made lobster salad overflowing a gourmet hot dog bun. The classic Rhode Island "grindah" is stuffed with sopressata, salami, mortadella, and mozzarella in a ciabatta roll.

Chef Roberts's fall menu is filled with autumnal delights. Pumpkin cheese on potato bread is griddled for a most unusual grilled cheese sandwich. The harvest salad combines fried pancetta, diced apples, fried onion strings, and greens dressed with apple cider vinaigrette. Come winter, egg sandwiches are made with trendy pretzel bread, and the hearty beef chili provides instant warmth. Soups are made on the premises, including a root vegetable soup with chicken and whole-grain elbows.

Tasting dinners are held at The Cafe on a monthly basis. A typical menu might start with Matunuck oysters, followed by mushroom-scented tagliatelle or chicken in phyllo. The Cafe does not have a liquor license so guests may bring their own wine or other alcoholic beverages.

CRAB CAKES, TWO WAYS

(MAKES 40 MINI CRAB CAKES)

8 ounces cream cheese

¾ cup grated Parmesan cheese

1 or 2 eggs

¼ cup sour cream

½ teaspoon lemon zest

¼ teaspoon salt

Pinch of cayenne pepper

1 cup panko bread crumbs

6 ounces lump crabmeat

Preheat oven to 350°F.

Option 1: In a bowl, combine all the ingredients (using just one egg), except the crabmeat. Fold in the crabmeat, being careful not to break the lumps. Form crab cakes in bite-size rounds. Heat a pan to medium-high, and spray lightly with nonstick pan spray. Sear the crab cakes lightly on both sides. Finish cooking the crab cakes in a 350°F oven for 15–20 minutes.

Option 2: In a bowl, combine all the ingredients (using just one egg), except the panko bread crumbs and crabmeat. Fold in the crabmeat, being careful not to break the lumps. In a separate bowl, mix the panko with a second egg. Spray mini muffin tins with nonstick pan spray. In each well, place a teaspoon of the panko-egg mixture and press into the bottom. Top with a teaspoon of the crab mixture. Bake at 350°F for 20–25 minutes.

BLUEBERRY BARBECUE SAUCE
OVER GRILLED CHICKEN

(MAKES 2 CUPS)

1 cup ketchup

¼ cup brown sugar

2 tablespoons white vinegar

1 tablespoon dry minced onion

2 tablespoons Worcestershire sauce

2 tablespoons mustard

2 cups blueberries

In a saucepan, combine all the ingredients. Stir to mix well. Heat slowly over medium-low heat until boiling. Simmer for 20 minutes. If desired, blend mixture with an immersion blender. Serve over grilled chicken.

Note: For a silkier consistency, strain the mixture through a fine sieve.

LEMON ZEST LOBSTER SALAD ROLLS

(MAKES 5 LOBSTER ROLLS)

¾ cup sour cream

¾ cup mayonnaise

½ lemon, juiced and zested

Salt and pepper, to taste

16 ounces lobster meat, cleaned and chopped roughly

5 hot dog buns (brioche buns are recommended)

5 ounces mesclun mixed greens

1 teaspoon chopped chives

In a bowl, mix together the sour cream, mayonnaise, lemon juice, and zest. Season to taste with salt and pepper. Gently toss the lobster meat with this dressing.

Toast the hot dog buns. Line each bun with the mixed greens. Evenly divide the lobster salad into the buns. Sprinkle with chopped chives.

CAMILLE'S

71 BRADFORD STREET
PROVIDENCE, RI 02903
(401) 751-4812
CAMILLESONTHEHILL.COM
EXECUTIVE CHEF JOHN GRANATA

One of the most talented chefs in Providence can be found at Camille's on Federal Hill, the Little Italy section of the city. Executive Chef John Granata is an expert when it comes to sophisticated Italian cuisine. It all started more than 20 years ago when Chef Granata worked as an "able apprentice" and then sous chef at Camille's. That's where his passion for classical Italian cooking took root. Chef Granata moved on, but returned to Camille's in 2002. His goal then was to restore Camille's to its former glory as one of the city's elite dining spots. Today he can proudly say, "Mission accomplished."

Opened in 1914, Camille's is celebrating its 100th year in business, making it the oldest Italian restaurant still in business in Rhode Island. This just may be the birthplace of fried calamari, the ubiquitous Italian appetizer found on almost every restaurant menu. Housed in a former mansion, the still elegant Camille's has always been the place

where celebrities dined while performing in Providence. The main attraction has been the impressive food and the impeccable service under the watchful eye of General Manager/ Sommelier Michael Degnan.

Camille's still has that old mansion feel. The heavy front door swings open, and you can either head for the dark lounge area, brightened by white leather seating, or the main dining room with its formally set tables and impressive chandeliers. Upstairs, in what used to be bedrooms, are private dining areas, ideal for major business deals and family gatherings. Camille's appeals to politicians and lawyers as well as the working man and his family.

The menu is written in Italian with English translations. The *calamari fritti* is Point Judith fried squid tossed with sliced banana peppers, Champagne garlic butter, and mint. Pasta dishes include the classic *pappardelle alla Bolognese,* a traditional slow-simmered three-meat sauce tossed with pasta ribbons, and Camille's famous lasagna, layered with Bolognese, ricotta, mozzarella, sausage, and meatballs. One of the most popular entrees is the aged filet mignon with Parmesan whipped potatoes and Barolo wine sauce.

Save room for dessert—you don't want to miss the lemon ricotta tartlet with blackberry compote or the hand-whipped Italian custard known as zabaglione.

SHRIMP & SCALLOPS OREGANATE

(SERVES 4–6)

½ pound butter, whipped

1 cup white wine, divided

¼ cup lemon juice

¼ cup plus 2 tablespoons red wine vinegar

2 tablespoons chopped parsley

1 pound capellini

6 jumbo Gulf shrimp

12 large sea scallops

Flour, as needed for dredging

½ cup extra-virgin olive oil

4 garlic cloves, chopped

½ cup chicken broth

1 teaspoon dried oregano

½ cup seasoned bread crumbs

½ cup grated Pecorino Romano cheese

Salt and pepper, to taste

If you are unable to purchase whipped butter, let the butter come to room temperature and whip it yourself with an electric mixer. Add ½ cup of wine, lemon juice, 2 tablespoons of vinegar, and parsley. Whip on medium speed until the butter turns white. Set aside.

In a pot of boiling salted water, cook the capellini until al dente.

Dredge the shrimp and scallops in the flour. In an oiled sauté pan, cook the seafood on both sides. Add the garlic, remaining ½ cup of wine, chicken broth, and the prepared whipped butter. Bring to a boil and reduce heat to a simmer. Add the oregano, bread crumbs, cheese, and remaining vinegar.

Toss this mixture with the cooked pasta. Season to taste with salt and pepper. Serve immediately.

Big Daddy Rib Eye Steak with Salsa Verde & Roasted Potato & Green Bean Salad

(SERVES 2)

Chef Granata's note: These steaks are so large that they could be cut in half, and then this recipe would serve four.

For the steaks:

2 (24-ounce) rib eye steaks, preferably 2 inches thick on the bone
2 tablespoons olive oil
1 tablespoon sea salt
1 teaspoon black pepper
1 teaspoon fennel seeds
1 teaspoon garlic powder
1 teaspoon rosemary
Salsa Verde (recipe follows)
Roasted Potato and Green Bean Salad (recipe follows)

For the salsa verde: (Makes about 2 cups)

½ cup chopped parsley
2 tablespoons chopped basil
1 tablespoon capers
4 anchovies
2 tablespoons chopped red onion
2 garlic cloves, chopped
1 tablespoon lemon juice
1 tablespoon red wine vinegar
½ cup extra virgin olive oil
Salt and pepper, to taste

For the roasted potato & green bean salad:
(Serves 4–6)

3 pounds red or Yukon Gold potatoes, cut in half
1 pound string beans, trimmed and cut in half
2 tablespoons olive oil
1 teaspoon kosher salt
4 bacon slices, cooked and chopped
2 cups diced Vidalia onions

1 garlic clove, minced
2 tablespoons Dijon mustard
4 tablespoons mayonnaise
1 tablespoon honey
2 tablespoons sherry vinegar
¼ cup chopped parsley
1 tablespoon chopped fresh dill
Salt and pepper, to taste
1 cup crumbled Gorgonzola cheese

To make the steaks: Brush the steaks with the oil. In a bowl, combine the salt, pepper, fennel, garlic powder, and rosemary, and mix well. Massage the steaks with the spice rub. Let the steaks sit in the refrigerator for 30 minutes. Preheat a grill. When the grill is ready, grill the steaks to desired doneness. Serve the steaks with the salsa verde and the roasted potato & green bean salad.

To make the salsa verde: In a bowl, combine all the ingredients.

To make the roasted potato & green bean salad: Preheat oven to 400°F.

Toss the potatoes and string beans in the olive oil, and season to taste with salt. Roast the potatoes and string beans in the 400°F oven for 45 minutes, turning the vegetables every 15 minutes, until tender. Allow the vegetables to cool to room temperature. Place the roasted vegetables in a large serving bowl. Mix in the remaining ingredients. Serve this salad at room temperature with the grilled steaks.

Zabaglione

(SERVES 2)

Chef Granata's note: Make sure the water is simmering, not boiling, or you will end up with scrambled eggs.

10 egg yolks
⅓ cup sugar
½ cup Marsala wine or Vin Santo
½ orange
Assorted summer berries
Dash of nutmeg (optional)

In a double boiler over simmering water, combine the first three ingredients all at once, constantly whipping the mixture with a wire whisk about 10 minutes, until it achieves a silky, fluffy, thick, pudding-like consistency.

When the custard is complete, immediately squeeze the juice from the half orange through a strainer into the custard. Mix well and spoon over the fresh berries in wine glasses. Sprinkle with nutmeg, if desired.

CAV

14 Imperial Place
Providence, RI 02903
(401) 751-9164
cavrestaurant.com
Chefs Alison Vanderburg and Josh Herring
Owner Sylvia Moubayed

CAV is unique. The word "restaurant" is French, from the verb *restaurer,* which means "to restore." And for the past 25 years, CAV has been doing what a restaurant by definition should do for its customers—restoring them with marvelous food and drink. The woman behind this extraordinary concept is Sylvia Moubayed, the grande dame of the Providence restaurant scene. Just about everyone knows Sylvia—like Elvis or Oprah, you need only speak her first name, and people immediately know who you're talking about. This Egyptian-born world traveler can be found at CAV every day, warmly greeting old and new customers, spending her precious time consoling them, mentoring them.

And then there's the remarkable food—this award-winning restaurant offers a sophisticated contemporary menu with international influences. The amazing food comes from a tiny kitchen with two chefs, currently Alison Vanderburg and Josh Herring, both graduates of the culinary school at Johnson & Wales University in Providence. CAV is a breeding ground for exceptional young chefs who hone their craft under Sylvia's tutelage.

The food at CAV is so well loved that Sylvia often finds it impossible to remove dishes from the menu to make room for new, exciting fare. CAV favorites include walnut-encrusted brie served warm with brandied sun-dried apricots, crostini with a mélange of wild mushrooms, and the white St. Donato pizza dotted with grilled chicken, artichokes, and Gorgonzola.

Sylvia wisely designs her seasonal menu in such a way that dining at CAV is possible for all, from local college students and struggling artists to well-to-do business people and suburbanites. A number of regular customers are from the Boston area, folks who are now hooked on CAV, in love with Sylvia and her attentive staff, and more than pleased with the affordable prices and free parking. The menu also offers plenty of vegetarian and gluten-free dishes.

CAV is open daily for lunch (think creative sandwiches and salads) and dinner (think butter-poached lobster and arguably the best filet mignon in the city) with an amazing brunch on weekends. Thick slices of french toast are topped with sautéed apples, raisins, and toasted nuts in a butterscotch maple sauce. Belgian waffles are kissed with strawberry-thyme syrup. Pistachio-encrusted crab cakes are served with a poached egg and grilled sweet bread.

And then there's the restaurant itself, housed in a historic building with a soaring ceiling and exposed beams. Colorful kilim rugs under glass cover every table, and tiny white lights dazzle the eye. CAV stands for "cocktails, antiques, and victuals." It takes a few minutes to take in all the artifacts, including pre-Columbian art, that are on display. Everything in this magical restaurant called CAV is for sale.

Butter-Poached Lobster with Tomato Bread Pudding & Fennel Salad

(SERVES 4)

For the butter-poached lobster:

4 lobsters, 1½ pounds each
Juice of 1 lemon
¼ cup thyme
¼ cup mirepoix (equal amounts of chopped onions, celery, and carrots)
¼ cup bay leaves
¼ cup juniper berries
1 tablespoon whole peppercorns
2 tablespoons melted butter

For the tomato bread pudding:

1 loaf Portuguese sweet bread
2 tomatoes, diced
4 eggs
1 cup heavy cream
2 tablespoons paprika

For the fennel salad:

2 fennel bulbs
Zest and juice of 1 orange
3 tablespoons olive oil
2 tablespoons melted butter
4 garlic cloves, chopped

For the beurre blanc:

8 tablespoons cold butter, cubed
1 shallot, minced
1 pinch saffron
1 cup white wine
2 cups heavy cream

To prepare the lobster: Poach each lobster in boiling water for 8 minutes. For added flavor, add the lemon juice, thyme, mirepoix, bay leaves, juniper berries, pepper, and butter to the water. Allow the lobsters to cool, then store in the refrigerator. If possible, loosen the lobster meat from its shell for easier eating.

To make the bread pudding: Preheat oven to 350°F. Cut the bread into 1-inch cubes. Place the bread cubes in a large mixing bowl. Add the diced tomatoes. In another bowl, whisk together the eggs, cream, and paprika. Pour the egg mixture over the bread cubes. Mix well. Pour this mixture into a greased 9 x 13-inch baking pan. Cover with aluminum foil and bake for 30 minutes in a 350°F oven. Remove the foil and bake for another 10 minutes.

To make the fennel salad: Slice the fennel bulbs lengthwise (using a mandoline for this task is recommended). Toss the sliced fennel in a bowl with the orange zest and juice and the olive oil.

To make the beurre blanc: Melt 1 teaspoon of butter in a saucepan over medium heat. Add the minced shallots and sweat (cook until softened). Lower the heat and add the saffron. Let steep for a few minutes. Deglaze the pan with the white wine and reduce. Add the cream and reduce. Turn off the heat. Slowly add the remaining cold butter piece by piece, whisking constantly. Be careful not to break this sauce by going too fast or adding too much butter.

To serve: In a large sauté pan, warm the poached lobster in melted butter.

In another sauté pan, warm the sliced fennel in melted butter and garlic.

To assemble: Cut the bread pudding into 4-inch squares. Place the bread pudding in the center of each serving plate. Top with some of the warm fennel salad. Top the salad with the poached lobster still in its colorful shell. Garnish the plate with a generous drizzle of the saffron beurre blanc.

Duck Confit with
Sweet Potato & Black Garlic–Peach Compote

(SERVES 2)

Chef Herring's note: This is a simplified method for preparing a complex dish. Duck fat can be purchased in gourmet meat markets. If impossible to find, you can use olive oil. Black garlic can be found at Whole Foods and Sid Wainer Specialty Foods.

For the duck:

4 duck legs
Duck fat (about 1 pound) or olive oil, as needed
¼ cup each of the following: rosemary, thyme,
    bay leaves, and black peppercorns
8 garlic cloves

For the garlic-peach compote:

1 cup blood orange juice
1 cup brandy
1 cup peach liqueur
3 tablespoons slurry (equal parts cornstarch and water)
Black garlic, at least 4 whole cloves or as many as
    you desire
3 fresh peaches, diced

For the sweet potatoes:

2 large sweet potatoes
4 tablespoons (½ stick) butter
4 tablespoons pure Vermont maple syrup
Salt and pepper, to taste

To make the duck: Preheat oven to 325°F.

In a deep baking pan, submerge the duck legs in enough duck fat or olive oil to cover, along with the herbs, spices, and garlic. Bake for 3 hours at 325°F. Let rest for 15 minutes.

To make the garlic-peach compote: In a saucepan, bring the blood orange juice, brandy, and peach liqueur to a simmer, and cook until reduced by half. Add the slurry and garlic, and stir until the sauce has a gravy texture. Add in the diced peaches. Remove from the heat and set aside.

To make the sweet potatoes: Peel and cut the sweet potatoes into chunks. In a pot, cover the sweet potatoes with water and boil until fork tender. Strain the water from the pot. Add the butter and maple syrup. Mash until smooth. Finish with salt and pepper to taste.

To plate: Place a generous serving of the mashed sweet potato in the center of each dinner plate. Top each with two duck legs so that the legs are standing up and crossed. Top the duck legs with some of the compote.

CHEZ PASCAL

960 HOPE STREET
PROVIDENCE, RI 02906
(401) 421-4422
CHEZ-PASCAL.COM
EXECUTIVE CHEF MATT GENNUSO

When Chez Pascal reopened with new owners in 2003, customers fell in love all over again, especially East Side residents who were regular patrons of this true neighborhood restaurant. Matt and Kristin Gennuso are now the talented husband-and-wife team in charge of the beloved Chez Pascal, with Matt as the executive chef and Kristin running the front of the house. They seem to do everything right at this mostly French bistro that gets rave reviews for its glowing ambience, satisfying food, and stellar service.

It's a cozy spot, quite romantic with soft lighting and formally set tables. You can dine at the bar or in the various dining nooks. The work of local artists is on display, changing every month or so. Even on a weeknight, it's not unusual for every table in this stylish restaurant to be taken.

Essentially Chez Pascal is still a French restaurant, but one that has embraced the use of local and seasonal ingredients whenever possible. Traditional escargots and onion soup gratiné coexist on the menu with Maine shrimp and smoked haddock chowder. The slow roasted half duck with sour cherry sauce vies for your attention along with the house-butchered pork of the day dish. Every season brings with it nuanced changes to the intriguing menu.

With that change in the season, outdoor cafe seating is available from spring into fall. One of the most pleasant dining experiences you can have is an early dinner at Chez Pascal on a warm autumn day with leaves of gold and red falling around your sidewalk table for two.

Chez Pascal is open only for dinner, but tucked into the corner of this successful business is the Wurst Kitchen, which serves wonderful sandwiches at lunchtime. You can dine inside at communal tables, or you can make use of the walk-up window to order house-made sausages done up creatively. My favorites include the smoked hot link with molasses baked beans and the kielbasa with crispy potato cake.

And if you can't make it over to 960 Hope Street, watch for the Chez Pascal food truck, called Hewtin's Dogs, which brings the Wurst Kitchen's sausages and sandwiches to various neighborhoods in Providence on an almost daily basis. Definitely worth trying are the house-made hot dogs and the bacon-wrapped pork meat loaf with spicy fig compote.

LEEK & POTATO CHOWDER WITH STUFFIE ROULADE

(SERVES 4–6)

Chef Gennuso's note: Milled potatoes are cooked potatoes that have been put through a food mill. They also can be pureed in an electric blender. Much like a vichyssoise, this soup may be served hot or cold.

For the chowder:

⅛ cup minced bacon

3 tablespoons butter

4 cups finely diced leek

1 cup finely diced onion

½ cup finely diced celery

2 cups finely diced potato (peeled)

Salt, to taste

2 cups milled cooked potato

3 tablespoons chopped thyme

3 quarts chicken stock

2 cups heavy cream

For the stuffie roulade:

36 littleneck clams, washed

2 bay leaves

1 small onion, sliced thin

1 cup dry white wine

8 tablespoons butter

½ cup minced chorizo, pre-cooked

¼ cup minced onion

¼ cup minced celery

¼ cup minced leeks

1 teaspoon fresh sage, chopped fine

1 teaspoon chopped parsley

1 teaspoon thyme

⅛ cup grated Parmesan cheese

1 quart fresh bread crumbs

1 lemon, zest removed and chopped

Paprika, for dusting

To make the chowder: In a 4-quart saucepan, render the bacon in the butter until it just begins to color. Add the leeks, onions, celery, and diced potatoes. Lightly season with salt. Cover the pan with a lid and cook over medium heat for 10 minutes or until the vegetables are tender and translucent. Add the milled cooked potato and chopped thyme. Cover the vegetables with the chicken stock and bring to a simmer. Simmer for about 1 hour and 30 minutes. Finish the soup with the heavy cream. Adjust to taste and either serve right away or chill until needed.

To make the stuffie roulade: Heat a 4-quart saucepan over medium heat for 2–3 minutes. When the pan is hot, carefully place the clams into the pot, then add the next three ingredients. Cover and let steam for 5–6 minutes, or until all the clams are open. Clams that refuse to open should be discarded.

Strain through a colander, making sure to save the strained liquid. Let the clams cool down. Remove the meat from each clam. Set the meat aside. You can discard the shells, or you can save them for use in another dish, in which case you should separate the shells and wash them thoroughly.

Melt the butter in a frying pan. Add the chorizo and lightly brown. Add the onions, celery, and leeks. Cover and cook until tender.

While the vegetables are cooking, finely chop the reserved clam meat. Set aside as this will be added to the filling at the end. Once the vegetables are tender, add in all the fresh herbs and heat, lightly toasting the herbs. Place this mixture into a large mixing bowl.

Add the chopped clam meat, Parmesan cheese, bread crumbs, and lemon zest. Mix everything with a spoon. The stuffing should be moist enough to hold together firmly. If it is too dry, use the reserved clam juice to moisten the stuffing.

To form the roulade: Place the stuffing mixture on a large sheet of plastic wrap. Roll into a roulade; that is, form the stuffing mixture into a roll and wrap tightly with the plastic wrap. Then wrap the roulade with aluminum foil to tighten the roulade. Refrigerate.

Allow to chill prior to slicing. To reheat, simply slice the roulade into quarter-inch discs.

Using a lightly oiled nonstick pan, sear the roulade slices on both sides until warm through the center. Use a roulade slice to garnish the center of each bowl of soup. Garnish with a dusting of paprika and, if desired, a littleneck clam that has been steamed open with the meat left inside.

Braised Pork Shoulder Roulade
with Salsa Verde
(SERVES 4–6)

Chef Gennuso's note: This dish can be served simply with roasted Yukon Gold potatoes and a salad of fresh greens.

For the pork shoulder:

1 (4- to 6-pound) pork shoulder roast
Salt and pepper, to taste
1 tablespoon blended oil
1 large onion, diced
2 carrots, diced
4 celery stalks, diced
2 garlic cloves, peeled and minced
1 tablespoon tomato paste
¼ cup red wine
Pinch of rosemary, thyme, and sage, chopped
2 cups veal stock
1 cup chicken stock
Salsa Verde (recipe follows)

For the salsa verde:

1 cup flat-leaf parsley leaves
3 tablespoons extra-virgin olive oil
⅛ cup minced shallots
2 tablespoons Champagne vinegar, or enough
    to cover the shallots
2 tablespoons chopped capers
Pinch of kosher salt

To make the pork shoulder: Place the roast on a cutting board. If the roast has been butterflied, open it up; if not, then butterfly it, and season with salt and pepper. Roll the shoulder into a roulade and tie with butcher's twine.

In a medium sauté pan, heat the blended oil to the smoking point. Season the outside of the roast with salt and pepper, and place it in the pan. Turn the roast, allowing it to brown on all sides without burning. Once this has been achieved, remove the roast from the pan and place into an ovenproof dish.

Preheat oven to 350°F.

In the same sauté pan, combine the onions, carrots, and celery, and lightly brown. Add the minced garlic followed by the tomato paste. Allow this mixture to cook briefly, then add the red wine and deglaze the pan. Allow the liquid to reduce to a paste, then add the herbs followed by the veal stock and chicken stock. Bring this liquid to a boil, pour over the roulade, and place in the preheated oven. Roast for approximately 2½ hours, or until it is tender throughout the roast. Be sure to continue to turn and baste the roulade as it cooks so it does not dry out.

Once it has cooked, remove the roulade from the oven and allow to sit at room temperature for about 20 minutes.

Once it is cool enough to handle, carefully remove the butcher's twine and slice the roulade as thinly as possible. These slices can be arranged on a platter and covered with foil to keep warm while the salsa verde is mixed.

To make the salsa verde: Pick the leaves from the stems of the parsley. Wash in cold water to remove any sand. Place in a salad spinner and dry. Using a mortar and pestle, pound the parsley leaves until they become a paste. If you do not have a mortar and pestle, a food processor will work. Once the parsley is pureed, cover with olive oil and set aside.

Add the shallots to the vinegar and allow to macerate for at least 1 hour. Strain the vinegar from the shallots. In a small mixing bowl, combine the strained shallots, parsley puree, and chopped capers. Lightly season the mixture with kosher salt, and drizzle over the sliced meat.

FARMERS' MARKETS

Not that many years ago, farmers' markets were a rarity in Rhode Island. In 2013, there were fifty-five farmers' markets across the state, from downtown Providence north to Woonsocket and south to Richmond. Farmers' markets used to open in late spring and close in mid-October, but now there are winter farmers' markets, which sustain those in search of farm-fresh produce. Farm Fresh Rhode Island is a local nonprofit organization that describes itself as "part incubator, part activator" when it comes to growing the local food system. Its mission is admirable—a New England abundant with diverse family farms and fertile soils, with locally and honestly produced foods and flavors at the heart of every dinner table. The website (farmfreshri.org) offers a wealth of information on where to find local food, Rhode Island farms, and farmers' markets.

Cook & Brown Public House

959 Hope Street
Providence, RI 02906
(401) 273-7275
COOKANDBROWN.COM
Executive Chef Nemo Bolin

Cook & Brown Public House is the kind of place where you'd be happy to dine every night of the week, if you could. Singles especially are very comfortable sitting at the bar, sipping on a cocktail while they wait for their dinner. This was what Chef Nemo Bolin envisioned in 2010 when he opened his small corner restaurant. Floor-to-ceiling plate glass windows provide a good glimpse inside at the mere eleven tables set up on the distressed wooden floor. The color scheme is neutral with pops of orange and an amazing basket-weave ceiling.

Chef Bolin's menu is devoted to New American cuisine, with a serious dedication to all things local and sustainable. The nightly menu is simple—six or seven seasonal items, plus another five specials that change daily. A typical menu might offer smoked bluefish and potato fritters with horseradish mayonnaise, a bowl of Maine mussels in a white wine and smoked fish broth, ricotta gnocchi, roasted chicken from a local farm, and sirloin steak from another local farm. That gnocchi is made with ricotta from Narragansett Creamery and is flavored in a number of ways; in the fall, it might be goat cheese, autumn vegetables, dried fruits, and walnuts. This is not your grandmother's gnocchi!

Desserts are a homey variety: creamy rice pudding with salted caramel, chocolate *pot de crème,* and a fragrant apple crisp for two.

Cook & Brown is known as much for its modern-day cocktails as for its honest food. Out-of-the-ordinary wines by the glass are available as well as intriguing beers, spirits, and after-dinner drinks. Wednesday night is especially popular with the "burger, beer, and bourbon" crowd, and family suppers are held every Sunday night, making Cook & Brown a right friendly place.

Swiss Chard Gratin

(SERVES 2)

Chef Bolin's note: At Cook & Brown, this is served in a small casserole dish for two people to share. The recipe can easily be doubled. For the grated cheese, Parmigiano-Reggiano is the best to use, but any hard Grana-style cheese will do. For the bread crumbs, leftover country bread smashed in the mortar and pestle is what we use at our restaurant.

2 garlic cloves

2 cups heavy cream

1 tablespoon unsalted butter

1 small onion, finely diced (⅛ inch)

12 swiss chard stems, finely diced (⅛ inch)

Salt, to taste

10–12 large leaves swiss chard, stems removed, roughly chopped

Kosher salt and freshly cracked black pepper, to taste

½ cup grated Parmesan cheese

¼ cup toasted bread crumbs

Combine the garlic cloves and heavy cream in a small saucepan over medium heat. Bring to a simmer. Keep an eye on it as the cream has a tendency to boil over. Slowly reduce the cream by half of its original volume. This should take about 30 minutes. Remove from the heat and mash the garlic with a spoon while still in the reduced cream. Set aside.

In a large sauté pan over medium heat, combine the butter, onions, and diced swiss chard stems. Season with salt, and continue to cook until the onions are soft and translucent. Add the chopped swiss chard leaves and season again with salt. Let the leaves wilt until reduced to half of their original size. Add the garlic and cream mixture, and continue cooking until the swiss chard is fully wilted and the cream is thick enough to coat the leaves without any excess in the pan. Season with salt and pepper to taste.

Place the swiss chard mixture in a gratin dish. Top with grated cheese and bread crumbs. Place under a broiler or in a hot oven until the cheese is completely melted and the top begins to brown slightly.

Ricotta Gnocchi

(SERVES 2)

Chef Bolin's note: The gnocchi must be frozen before they can be cooked, so the gnocchi must be made in advance. We recommend using the ricotta from Narragansett Creamery. At our restaurant, we change the accompaniments for the gnocchi every six weeks or so to stay in tune with the seasons. It is almost always a vegetarian dish.

1 quart very fresh ricotta
2 eggs
Salt, to taste
1 cup all-purpose flour

In a food processor, combine the ricotta, eggs, and salt until well mixed. Add the flour slowly until a soft dough forms. Depending on the moisture level of the ricotta, all of the flour may not be needed. Less flour will be better, yielding lighter gnocchi.

Test in boiling salted water. That is, with a small spoon, scoop some of this ricotta mixture and form into a single, firm gnocchi. Drop the gnocchi into a small pan of boiling water. The gnocchi

should hold together. If it starts to fall apart, you will need to add a little flour and then test again.

Place the ricotta mixture in a pastry bag. Pipe to desired size on a parchment-lined sheet pan. Place the sheet pan in the freezer until frozen through.

Directly from the freezer, place the frozen gnocchi in boiling salted water. Lower the heat to a simmer. Cook until the gnocchi float and are barely cooked through, approximately 5 minutes.

With a slotted spoon, remove the floating gnocchi from the pot of water. Place the gnocchi in a bowl. They are now ready to be sauced in any way you choose.

Costantino's Venda Ravioli, Venda Caffe, and Venda Bar & Ristorante

Depasquale Plaza
265-275 Atwells Avenue
Providence, RI 02903
(401) 421-9105
vendaravioli.com
Chef Salvatore Cefaliello
Chef Giovanni Ricci
Chef Anthony Chiero

Costantino's—that family name is the symbol of authentic Italian food in Providence, Rhode Island. And the Costantino family delivers that authentic Italian food via three ways: Venda Ravioli, which includes Venda's catering division, Venda Caffe, and Venda Bar & Ristorante, all located on Federal Hill (Little Italy). Each venue has its own executive chef.

Venda Ravioli is an Italian food emporium where all things Italian can be purchased: prepared foods, deli items, high-quality meats, a vast assortment of imported olives, more than 150 international cheeses, gourmet products including espresso, and the house specialty, fresh pasta. Within this busy market is an equally busy Italian caffè where the magnificent food is prepared by Chef Salvatore Cefaliello, who returns every

year to his native Italy in search of new dishes to share with his many regular customers back in America. Pasta dishes showered with freshly shaved truffles and *linguine alla bottarga* are just two of his specialties.

The colorful to-go prepared foods are the work of Chef Giovanni Ricci, who also oversees the catering division of Venda Ravioli. His classic pasta dishes, savory entrees, and tempting desserts often evoke a "wow" response from clients.

If you like Venda Ravioli, you will love Venda Bar & Ristorante on the other side of DePasquale Plaza. Chef Anthony Chiero, who apprenticed under Chef Salvatore, is in charge of this beautiful Italian restaurant with seating on two levels plus alfresco dining in warm weather. His creations are not only elegant but delicious as well, from the creamy *burrata e prosciutto* drizzled with extra-virgin olive oil to the *saltimbocca alla Romana*. Venda's famous freshly made pastas play an important role on the menu with the lobster ravioli being Chef Anthony's signature dish.

When Rhode Islanders move away and they are asked what they miss most about their little state, more often than not they simply say: "Venda."

LINGUINE ALLA BOTTARGA

(SERVES 4)

Chef Salvatore's note: *Bottarga* is the salted, pressed, and dried roe of gray mullet (*muggine*) or tuna (*tonno*). It is a specialty of both Sardinia and Sicily. To make bottarga, the entire fat roe sac is salted and massaged by hand over several weeks to eliminate air pockets. The roe is then pressed and sun-dried for one to two months. Hence the high price of bottarga, which is available in gourmet markets and online (chefshop-gourmet-food-store.com). Packages of bottarga can range from 3 to 10 ounces, with a price range of $32 to $80.

1 gallon water or more, for boiling pasta
1 pound fresh linguine from Venda Ravioli
2 tablespoons extra-virgin olive oil
1 large garlic clove, minced
1 pinch hot pepper seeds, more or less to taste
5 parsley sprigs, minced
1 tablespoon grated Pecorino Romano
1 (6-ounce) package of bottarga di muggine

Bring the lightly salted water to a boil for cooking the linguine. Add the linguine to the boiling water and cook for approximately 4–6 minutes, until al dente.

While the linguine is cooking, add the extra-virgin olive oil, garlic, and hot pepper seeds to a large sauté pan over medium high heat. (A 10-inch pan is recommended.) Cook until the garlic begins to lightly brown. Add ¼ cup of pasta water to the pan to stop the garlic from burning.

When the pasta is al dente, drain and reserve some of the pasta water. Add the pasta to the sauté pan with the parsley and grated cheese. With a cheese grater, grate half of the bottarga into the pasta and toss everything together. If necessary, add a few more spoonfuls of pasta water to the sauté pan to create a little sauce and moisten the pasta.

Distribute pasta equally among 4 pasta bowls. Grate the rest of the bottarga over each pasta dish to finish.

Capicola Arrosto over Creamy Polenta

(SERVES 6–8)

Chef Giovanni's note: This roasted pork is one of my favorite dishes to make on a snowy day. Boston pork butt is always available at local markets and especially at small specialty shops at very reasonable prices. It's often used in making sausage and cold cuts, and rarely used as an entrée, until now in this dish. This recipe should be made in advance so that a proper sauce can be prepared.

For the pork:

3- to 4-pound pork butt

Salt and black pepper, as needed

Crushed red pepper, as needed

Olive oil, as needed

3–4 leaves fresh sage, finely chopped

1 sprig fresh rosemary, leaves removed and chopped

Seasoned flour, as needed

1 large onion, cut into julienne strips

3 cups beef stock

1 pat butter, dusted with flour

Creamy Polenta (recipe follows)

For the polenta:

2 cups chicken stock

Salt and pepper, to taste

2 cups whole milk

1 cup finely ground cornmeal

1 tablespoon black truffle oil

To make the pork: Cut the pork butt in half, then into 8–10 pieces, leaving them from 1½ to 2 inches thick. Massage the pork pieces generously with salt, black pepper, crushed red pepper, olive oil, and half of the sage and rosemary. Lightly roll the pork pieces in flour. Allow the pork pieces to sit for 30 minutes on wax paper.

Heat a medium-sized sauté pan. Add enough olive oil to coat the bottom of the pan. Once the oil is hot, gently place three or four pieces of pork in the pan, and brown on both sides. Place the browned pieces in a roasting pan. Repeat until all the pork is in the pan.

Toss the onions in flour that has been seasoned with salt and pepper. Add the onions to the roasting pan around each piece of meat.

Preheat oven to 350°F.

In a saucepan, heat the beef stock with the remainder of the sage and rosemary. Pour this mixture into the roasting pan, and cover the pan tightly with foil. Place the pan in the preheated oven and roast for 2½ hours. Remove the pan from the oven and let sit fully wrapped for another 30 minutes.

To make the sauce: Using a spatula, carefully remove the meat from the pan and set aside on a platter. Strain the juice from the roasting pan. Chill the juice so the oil congeals, and discard the oil. Reheat the sauce and add a pat of floured butter. Stir well over low heat until ready to serve.

To make the polenta: In a heavy-bottomed saucepan, bring the chicken stock to a boil, and add the salt and pepper to your taste. Once the salt has dissolved, add the milk and return the mixture to a simmer.

Slowly add the cornmeal and whisk it in as you pour. Continue to stir every few minutes for about a half hour. If it starts to become to firm, add more milk.

In the last few minutes of cooking, add the truffle oil and whisk in well. Cover the saucepan, and allow the polenta to sit off the heat for a few minutes.

To plate this dish: Cover the bottom of each dinner plate with some of the polenta. Place one or two pieces of meat on top, and drizzle with the warm sauce.

Tortellini alla Panna

(SERVES 4)

Chef Anthony's note: Mama's Home-Style tortellini is available at Venda Ravioli (vendaravioli.com).

2 tablespoons butter

2 garlic cloves, minced

¼ pound prosciutto di Parma or prosciutto cotto (cooked ham), sliced into thin strips

½ cup chicken stock

1 cup heavy cream

1 pound cheese tortellini (Mama's Home-Style is recommended)

Pinch fresh chopped parsley

1 pinch nutmeg, freshly grated (optional)

¾ cup fresh English peas or frozen green peas (optional)

¼ cup freshly grated Parmigiano-Reggiano

Salt and pepper, to taste

Bring about 1 gallon of lightly salted water to a boil to cook the tortellini.

In a sauté pan, combine the butter, garlic, and prosciutto, and cook over medium-high heat. Allow the prosciutto to slightly crisp and the garlic to soften, 3–5 minutes. Add the chicken stock and reduce by half over high heat, 3–5 minutes. Add the heavy cream and allow to reduce by ¼, then turn off the heat.

Cook the tortellini for 6–8 minutes in the boiling water. When the tortellini are al dente, transfer them to the cream sauce in the sauté pan, and return the pan to medium-high heat. Add the parsley, nutmeg, English peas, and grated Parmigiano-Reggiano. Toss gently and allow the sauce to thicken around the tortellini. Season to taste with salt and pepper.

GRACIE'S

194 WASHINGTON STREET
PROVIDENCE, RI 02903
(401) 272-7811
GRACIESPROVIDENCE.COM
EXECUTIVE CHEF MATTHEW VARGA
PASTRY CHEF MELISSA DENMARK

You'll see stars when you dine at Gracie's, both kinds of stars. Stars are part of the sophisticated motif at this downtown restaurant. Stars appearing across the street at Trinity Repertory Theater often dine at Gracie's, and with good reason. This is simply one of the finest restaurants in Providence. The food and service are impeccable.

Matthew Varga is the chef/magician who makes it all happen. His ingredient combinations defy reason, but every dish is a success. For starters, who else would think to pair peaches and tomatoes in a salad? But Chef Varga doesn't stop there. Supporting roles in that salad include stracciatella cheese, shaved radish, garden herbs and flowers dressed with aged balsamic vinegar. The foie gras on the menu always has a seasonal element—in the summer it's teamed up with blueberries, lemon curd, and corn bread.

For the main course, Chef Varga offers duck with blue cheese potato croquettes, baby fennel, glazed onions, and Bing cherries. His all-natural New York strip steak is presented with roasted bone marrow, bok choy, king oyster mushrooms, and charred scallions.

Extraordinary desserts from Pastry Chef Melissa Denmark are dazzling, from a lemon tart served with beach rose jam and honeysuckle ricotta ice cream to the crème brûlée made with vanilla beans from Madagascar.

For a real treat, make reservations for one of the chef's tastings, pricey but well worth it. Five-course and seven-course dinners paired with appropriate wines are available, as well as a three-course dessert tasting for guests with a serious sweet tooth.

Chef Varga's insider tip: At Gracie's, there is a very special table for two that's often reserved for momentous occasions, such as marriage proposals. The intimate table, impeccably set with crystal stemware and sparkling candlelight, is tucked behind half walls that ensure totally private conversations and displays of affection.

Rhode Island Striped Bass
with Heirloom Tomatoes & Garden Beans

(SERVES 4)

3 tablespoons vegetable oil

1½ pounds striped bass fillets, skin on, cut into
    4 equal pieces

Salt, to taste

2 tablespoons butter

¼ teaspoon Dijon mustard

1 tablespoon verjus (juice of unripened grapes,
    available in gourmet stores)

1 tablespoon chopped herbs (parsley, chervil, chives)

Salt and pepper, to taste

3 tablespoons olive oil

4 mixed heirloom tomatoes, cut into quarters

8 ounces green beans, blanched

2 radishes, thinly sliced

1 shallot, sliced lengthwise

Garden herbs and flowers, for garnish

1 tablespoon dried black olives, crushed

Preheat oven to 350°F.

Place a large sauté pan over high heat. Add the vegetable oil. Season the fish fillets on both sides with salt. Place the fish fillets in the hot pan skin side down. Lower heat to medium-high. Cook until golden brown, 2–3 minutes. Add the butter to the pan. Turn the fish fillets to flesh side down. Baste for the next 30 seconds or so. Move the fish fillets into the oven for about 5 minutes, or until an internal temperature of 135–140°F is reached. Allow the fish to rest for 2–3 minutes before serving.

In a small bowl, whisk together the mustard, verjus, herbs, and a pinch of salt and pepper.

Slowly add the olive oil to make a vinaigrette. Set aside.

In a bowl, combine the tomatoes, beans, radishes, and shallot. Season to taste with salt and pepper. Add the vinaigrette and mix well. Allow to marinate for 2–3 minutes.

To serve, prepare four dinner plates with an equal amount of the tomato mixture on each. Place a piece of striped bass on each plate. Garnish with garden herbs and flowers. Finish with a generous sprinkle of the dried olives.

Honey-Roasted Beets
with Hannahbells Cheese & Marcona Almonds
(SERVES 6)

Chef Varga's note: It's best to peel the red beets last and store them in a separate container. Their red color will stain the other beets.

For the beets:

3 baby red beets

3 baby golden beets

3 baby candy-striped beets

1 cup sherry vinegar

1 cup water

3 tablespoons Aquidneck Island honey, or any local honey

2 tablespoons olive oil

2 teaspoons salt

Vinaigrette (recipe follows)

6 ounces baby arugula, washed

Salt and freshly cracked black pepper, to taste

3 tablespoons chopped Marcona almonds

12 Hannahbells cheeses (exclusively from Shy Brothers Farm in Westport, Mass.)

For the vinaigrette: (Makes ⅔ cup)

¼ cup olive oil

¼ cup vegetable oil

1 tablespoon sherry vinegar

1 tablespoon white wine vinegar

¼ teaspoon Dijon mustard

1 teaspoon minced shallots

1 teaspoon lemon juice

1 teaspoon Aquidneck Island honey

To make the beets: Preheat oven to 350°F.

In a large bowl, combine the beets, sherry vinegar, water, 2 tablespoons honey, olive oil, and salt. Mix well. Place the mixture in a 2-inch deep roasting pan. Bake for 45 minutes. You should be able to pierce the beets easily with a paring knife or cake tester. Remove the beets from the oven. Allow to cool slightly. While they are still warm, peel the beets with a paper towel.

Cut each beet into four bite-size pieces. Allow the beets to cool completely in the refrigerator.

To make the vinaigrette: Combine all the ingredients in a food processor and blend until incorporated. Season to taste with salt and freshly cracked black pepper. You will need only some of this vinaigrette, which can be stored in the refrigerator for future use.

In a mixing bowl, combine the arugula with 3 tablespoons of the vinaigrette. Toss to coat evenly. Season to taste with salt and pepper. Divide the dressed greens evenly among 6 chilled salad plates.

To the same mixing bowl, add the golden and candy-striped beets with 2–3 tablespoons of vinaigrette. Toss to coat evenly. Place 2 of each color beets onto each salad plate.

To the same mixing bowl, add the red beets and 2–3 tablespoons of the vinaigrette. Toss to coat evenly. Place 2 pieces of red beets on each salad plate.

Drizzle each salad with the remaining honey. Sprinkle the chopped almonds over the beets. Place two pieces of cheese on each plate. Finish each salad with freshly cracked black pepper.

THE GRANGE

166 BROADWAY
PROVIDENCE, RI 02903
(401) 831-0600
PROVIDENCEGRANGE.COM
EXECUTIVE CHEF JON DILLE

The Grange calls itself "a vegetable restaurant, cafe, and bar." Local vegetarians have fallen in love with this quirky eatery. Surprisingly many of The Grange's biggest fans are not vegetarians. All you have to do is stop in for lunch or dinner and try two or three items on the menu. It's likely you will find everything honestly delicious.

The Grange is the latest chapter in the story of Rob and Ursula Yaffe, owner of the Garden Grille vegetarian restaurant and Wildflour Vegan Bakery, Cafe and Juice Bar, both in nearby Pawtucket. Their mission is to provide people with alternative, healthier choices in cooking and eating. Also devoted to a more wholesome way of living is Jon Dille, executive chef at The Grange. A native of Pennsylvania, Dille holds a bachelor's degree in nutrition from Johnson & Wales University's College of Culinary Arts. He's determined to elevate diners' perceptions of a vegetarian diet. His menu, which emphasizes seasonal, organic produce from local farms, is short but delicious. Every Thursday, three to seven items on the menu change.

A typical menu might include a soup served with bread from Foremost Bakery. The goat cheese deviled eggs are a real treat, topped with pickled jalapeño and fried shallots.

Other dishes that are fun to share include *pommes frites* with aioli, grilled corn with miso butter, sautéed greens with raisins and pistachios, wok-fried pole beans, and quinoa with creamy avocado dressing.

Larger plates feature that French-Canadian specialty, poutine; here it's a pile of *pommes frites* with mushroom gravy, cheese, and chives. The po-boy is stuffed with chicken fried oyster mushrooms. Korean BBQ tacos are made with seitan. Sandwiches include crispy sesame tofu and fried green tomatoes with interesting accompaniments. The bowls of warm soba noodles, coconut dhal curry, and roasted vegetables are hearty and satisfying.

Healthy eating does not mean you have to give up everything you love. This corner restaurant also offers colorful drinks such as mint lemonade and wonderful desserts. Classic cocktails are whipped up by bartender extraordinaire Joe Haggard, all in an appealing shabby-chic setting. The 100-percent repurposed interior features lots of hand-me-down furniture, even an old-fashioned porch swing.

Coffee enthusiasts claim the best can be found in Chicory, the quaint coffee and juice bar located inside The Grange, with its own separate entrance for to-go orders. Open daily at 8 a.m., Chicory serves Stumptown Coffee as well as all-natural juices and vegan/gluten-free breakfast pastries and desserts. Make sure you try the beignets.

(The Garden Grille and the Wildflour Vegan Bakery, Cafe, and Juice Bar are both located in a shopping plaza at 727 East Avenue in Pawtucket, Rhode Island.)

THE SIREN'S MUSE
(MAKES 1 COCKTAIL)

2 ounces Vida mezcal
½ ounce Green Chartreuse
¼ ounce Benedictine
3 dashes orange bitters
1 twist of grapefruit zest

Combine all the liquid ingredients, and strain the mixture into a coupe glass. Top with the grapefruit zest. Serve immediately.

ROASTED CAULIFLOWER WITH TWO SAUCES

(SERVES 2)

For the cauliflower:

2 small to medium heads cauliflower, various
    colors preferred
Canola oil, as needed
Salt, to taste
Ginger scallion sauce (recipe follows)
Cilantro ginger sauce (recipe follows)
Very thin slices of turnips and radishes, for garnish
Toasted pumpkin seeds, for garnish

For the ginger scallion sauce: (Makes 1–2 cups)

½ cup peeled and roughly chopped ginger
3 bunches scallions
¼ cup rice vinegar
¼ cup water
Salt, to taste

For the cilantro ginger sauce: (Makes 1–2 cups)

1 bunch cilantro, washed and chopped fine
¼ cup peeled and minced ginger root
1 cup Vegenaise (egg-free mayonnaise)
    or regular mayonnaise
Pinch of salt and white pepper

To make the ginger scallion sauce: Place all the ingredients in a food processor. Puree until smooth and pieces are small and uniform in size. Taste and season with more salt, if needed, and set aside.

To make the cilantro ginger sauce: Place all the ingredients in a mixing bowl. Whisk together. Set aside for plating.

To make the roasted cauliflower: Preheat oven to 450°F.

Cut the cauliflower into 1-inch florets. Toss the cauliflower in a large bowl with the oil. Sprinkle with salt. Place the cauliflower on a baking sheet. Roast in the 450°F oven until lightly browned and just tender, 15–20 minutes. Remove the cauliflower from the baking sheet and place in a large bowl. Coat with the ginger scallion sauce.

To serve, place some of the cilantro ginger sauce on the bottom of a serving plate. Place the cauliflower on the plate. Garnish with the turnips, radishes, and pumpkin seeds.

Harry's Bar & Burger

121 North Main Street
Providence, RI 02903
(401) 228-7437
HARRYSBARBURGER.COM
Maestro John Elkhay

Harry's is one of the smallest restaurants in Providence, but it's big on flavor and fun. The life-size black-and-white cow on the sidewalk in front of Harry's is your first sign that this is a restaurant that does not take itself too seriously. But Harry's does offer seriously good food made with fresh ingredients from local purveyors.

This popular bar that is known for its mini burgers (aka sliders) is part of the Chow Fun Food Group, the dynasty created by John Elkhay, a local lad who grew up to be one of the city's most accomplished and successful chefs. Known as The Maestro, Elkhay has evolved into a cutting-edge restaurateur, but he still collaborates with his chefs when it comes time to create new menu items. Harry's is named after son Harrison Elkhay, who is often seen there behind the bar serving up a craft beer or two. Harry's tiny kitchen is turning out burgers that have been deemed among the best in the nation by *Travel + Leisure* magazine.

Those burgers are made with pure Hereford beef, freshly ground, never frozen, handmade daily, and all topped with the house special sauce. The basic burger with grilled onions is the base for almost a dozen variations on that theme, from an unusual pastrami slider to burgers topped with spicy chili, pulled pork, or fried onion strings. The fanciest entree is a burger topped with portobello mushrooms and truffle aioli.

Jumbo hot dogs, creative sandwiches, and all kinds of munchies round out the festive menu. The huge selection of craft beers is sourced locally and from around the world.

Insider tip: All the burgers are half price every day from 3 to 5 p.m.

Pastrami Burger Sliders

(SERVES 4)

For the burgers:

8 Martin's Potato Dinner Rolls
8 tablespoons Special Sauce (recipe follows)
1 cup shredded lettuce
8 pickle slices
1 pound ground beef, divided into 2-ounce portions
1 cup chopped yellow onions
4 slices American cheese, cut in half
8 ounces black pastrami, warmed and chopped

For the Special Sauce: (Makes ¾ cup)

½ cup mayonnaise
¼ cup ketchup
1 tablespoon mustard
½ teaspoon dried tarragon

To make the Special Sauce: In a mixing bowl, mix all ingredients until well blended.

To make the burgers: Place the bottom buns on a serving plate, and top each with 1 tablespoon of special sauce, a pinch of shredded lettuce, and a pickle slice.

In a large skillet over medium-high heat, add the burger patties. Place about 2 tablespoons of the chopped onions on top of the meat. With a large metal spatula, "smash" the burgers flat, pressing the onions into the meat. Cook for about 1–2 minutes, then flip the burgers over. Immediately add ½ slice cheese to each burger. Place the top bun on top of each burger so it can steam. Cook for about 30 seconds more.

Place 2 tablespoons of the warm pastrami on top of each bottom bun on the serving plate. When the burgers are finished cooking, place them on the prepared buns and serve. Allow two sliders per person.

HEMENWAY'S SEAFOOD GRILL & OYSTER BAR

121 SOUTH MAIN STREET
PROVIDENCE, RI 02903
(401) 351-8570
HEMENWAYSRESTAURANT.COM
EXECUTIVE CHEF LEE SONSKY

One of Providence's most enduring restaurants, Hemenway's Seafood Grill & Oyster Bar is known for its impeccable seafood flown in daily from around the world and locally sourced from Point Judith, Rhode Island, and other New England fishing ports. For more than 20 years, Hemenway's has been the go-to restaurant for special occasions and important business meetings. It is now part of the prestigious Newport Restaurant Group.

Located next to the Providence River and Market Square Park, Hemenway's is in big demand on WaterFire nights, when the river is ablaze with small bonfires and gondolas glide by. In its own right, this multilevel restaurant is dazzling to the eye with its colorful neon and a fishing boat that hangs from the ceiling. In addition to a busy bar, there's an oyster bar where oyster lovers can sit and watch their oysters being shucked by skillful hands. With a glass of white wine, this is the perfect prelude to an outstanding dinner.

Lee Sonsky is the executive chef at Hemenway's. He got his start at a small Italian restaurant on Long Island and then spent twelve years at the prestigious Breakers in Palm Beach, Florida.

Chef Sonsky's menu features classic dishes as well as innovative items. Under New England traditions, diners can find the traditional scrod, sea scallops, whole belly clams, and Alaskan king crab legs. The Maine lobster is stuffed with a mixture of shrimp, scallops, and crab. The chef's specialties include pan-seared halibut with vegetable hash, salmon with spinach couscous, and paella overflowing with shrimp, scallops, clams, and mussels. Landlubbers can dine on filet mignon, New York strip steak, lemon-herb marinated chicken, and brined pork rib chop.

Hemenway's is especially known for its fabulous Oyster Festival held every September in the adjacent park. Admission is free to the afternoon event which features music from a steel drum band. Food and drink tickets are sold to attendees hungry for oysters from New England and Canada. Plenty of other shellfish, seafood pasta, grilled pizza, and desserts are also available. The festival is a benefit for Save the Bay, which is dedicated to protecting the ecological health of Narragansett Bay.

Approximately half a million oysters have been served at Hemenway's over the past two decades.

JONAH CRAB ESCABECHE SALAD

(SERVES 1)

Chef Sonsky's note: This recipe can easily be doubled.

3 very thin slices English cucumber, cut lengthwise

1½ cups mixed greens

3 tablespoons diced mango

2 tablespoons diced cucumber

1 tablespoon diced red onion

1 tablespoon torn cilantro leaves

1 tablespoon diced red bell pepper

3 cherry tomatoes, cut in half

4 ounces Jonah crabmeat, preferably claw meat

¼ cup citrus marinade (recipe follows)

Salt and pepper, to taste

Pinch Hawaiian pink sea salt, for garnish

For the citrus marinade: (Makes 2 cups)

1 cup orange juice

½ cup lime juice

½ cup rice wine vinegar

½ jalapeño pepper, seeds removed, minced

½ teaspoon red pepper flakes

1½ teaspoons kosher salt

2 tablespoons sugar

To make the citrus marinade: Combine all ingredients, and stir with a whisk until the salt and sugar are absorbed.

To make the salad: Lay the thin slices of cucumber out flat on a salad plate. The salad will be built on top of these slices.

In a mixing bowl, combine all other ingredients (except the sea salt), being careful not to break up the crabmeat too much. Arrange the mixed salad on top of the cucumber slices, trying to leave the colorful components on top. Pour the remaining liquid over the exposed parts of the cucumber slices. Sprinkle the salad with the pink sea salt.

Paella with Saffron Rice

(SERVES 2)

Chef Sonsky's note: Calasparra rice is the rice traditionally used in a paella. If not available, you can use any short-grain rice. This rice dish can be done a few hours in advance. It should make more than enough rice for two servings.

¼ cup small diced yellow onion

1 teaspoon canola oil

1½ cups chicken broth

1 pinch saffron

1 cup Calasparra rice

1 tablespoon kosher salt

1 pinch black pepper

2 teaspoons canola oil

8 littleneck clams

6 ounces swordfish medallions

24 jumbo sea scallops

½ cup chopped chorizo, cut into ¼-inch pieces

12 mussels

6 tail-on shrimp, medium to large

Salt and pepper, to taste

½ cup vegetable stock

2 cups cooked saffron rice (recipe follows)

4 tablespoons chopped pimientos

2 tablespoons sliced scallions

To make the saffron rice: Preheat oven to 350°F.

In a small saucepan, slowly cook the diced onion in the canola oil until the onions are soft and fragrant (it is important not to caramelize the onions). Add the chicken broth and saffron. Bring to a boil and then shut off the heat. Let it steep for 10 minutes.

In a baking pan at least a half-inch deep, spread the rice on the bottom. Turn the heat back on the chicken broth mixture. Once it returns to a boil, pour it over the rice. Cover the pan tightly with aluminum foil and bake in the preheated oven for 14 minutes, or until 95 percent of the liquid is absorbed. Season to taste with salt and pepper. Cool and reserve until you make the paella.

To make the paella: Heat the canola oil in a large sauté pan over medium heat. Season all the seafood and meat with salt and pepper on both sides. Add the clams, swordfish, and scallops to the pan, and sear on both sides to a dark golden brown. Then add the chorizo, mussels, and shrimp.

Once the chorizo starts to brown, deglaze the pan with the vegetable stock. Once the clams and mussels are open, add the saffron rice to the pan. Once incorporated, add the pimientos and scallions. Adjust the seasoning with salt and pepper as needed.

To plate, place the rice in the middle of two serving bowls and arrange the shellfish around the outside of the rice. Place the remaining seafood and chorizo on top of the rice.

Before Perry Raso opened the wildly successful Matunuck Oyster Bar, he was an oyster farmer. With college degrees in aquaculture and fisheries technology, he founded the seven-acre Matunuck Oyster Farm in 2002. The farm is within Potter Pond in East Matunuck, adjacent to Perry's restaurant and raw bar. The farm supplies the restaurant with fresh oysters being harvested just beyond the waterfront patio. Some restaurants have a "farm to table" philosophy when it comes to food. Matunuck Oyster Bar has a "pond to plate" concept, offering simple food made with fresh, local products at a reasonable price. Raso grows it. He harvests it. And he serves it.

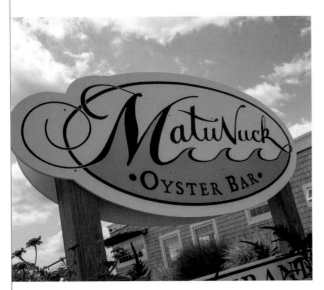

Tours of the oyster farm, which include lunch at the restaurant, are available. Raso personally conducts the ninety-minute tours, which start with a discussion of the local barrier beach, salt marsh, and estuary. Participants then don professional waders so they can wade on into the shellfish farm with Raso leading the way. This unusual field trip teaches participants how shellfish are cultivated in local waters.

For a tour schedule and pricing, call (401) 783-4202, or send an e-mail to matunuckoyster bar@gmail.com.

Matunuck Oyster Farm is one of several now operated in the waters in and around the Rhode Island coastline. Others are Cedar Island Oyster Farm, East Beach Farm, East Beach Oyster Company, Ninigret Oyster Farm, and Rome Point Oyster Farm. All six are members of the Ocean State Shellfish Cooperative.

JULIAN'S

318 BROADWAY
PROVIDENCE, RI 02909
(401) 861-1770
JULIANSPROVIDENCE.COM
CHEF DAVID SPINGOLD

One of the most unusual restaurants in Providence, Julian's is a reflection of owner Julian Forgue's unique personality. First of all, there is no sign outside this corner restaurant, but it's easy to find. Just look for the mechanical hobbyhorse on the sidewalk, a relic from the 1950s (and it still works). Under a deep red awning are wrought-iron tables and chairs for alfresco dining. But make sure you venture inside this dark, bohemian cafe where the decor is as quirky as the clientele. Artists, vegans, anyone with an alternative lifestyle likes to spend time with their friends at Julian's. And do visit the restroom, where the owner's massive Pez candy dispenser collection is on display behind glass.

The menu is equally odd, but thoroughly delicious with Chef David Spingold in the kitchen. When the talented chef brainstorms with the outside-of-the-box owner, original dishes are created and then evolve into something extraordinary. That is the case with their boneless roast leg of lamb that is flavored with whole-grain mustard and chopped pistachios. A Marrakesh spice blend is used to season the accompanying orzo, and the dish is garnished with fresh figs and tiny pickled cucumbers found at a local farmer's market.

Other intriguing creations include a strawberry-rhubarb pizza with Manchego cheese, fresh zucchini blossoms stuffed with Chinese five-spiced rice, and Creole-style seared tofu with pineapple glaze. The beer-battered local cod might sound almost ordinary, but it's served with Cajun fingerling fries and cilantro-curry mayo.

If you can't make it to Julian's, the catering division of Julian's will go to your house—in a British double-decker bus.

Since Julian's opened in 1994, this imaginative restaurant has been serving lunch, dinner, and an especially popular weekend brunch. Often, there's a line of customers out on the sidewalk next to that hobbyhorse, but dining at Julian's is definitely worth the wait.

Roasted Leg of Lamb with Lemon-Dill Greek Yogurt Sauce

(SERVES 8–10)

For the lamb:

3- to 4-pound boneless leg of lamb

½ cup minced garlic

2 tablespoons chopped fresh oregano

¾ cup whole-grain mustard

1 cup toasted pistachios, roughly chopped

Salt and pepper, to taste

For the lemon-dill Greek yogurt sauce: (Makes 1 cup)

1 cup Greek yogurt

Zest and juice from 1 lemon

¼ bunch dill, chopped

Salt and white pepper, to taste

To make the lamb: Trim the fat and silver skin off the lamb leg and cut it open, butterflying it as much as possible. Rub the lamb with garlic and oregano. Wrap the lamb with plastic wrap and refrigerate overnight (or at least 4–6 hours, but the longer the better).

Take the lamb out of the refrigerator. Rub it with the mustard and sprinkle with the pistachios. Roll tightly and truss using butcher twine, tying it as tightly as possible.

Preheat the oven to 425°F.

Place the lamb on a roasting rack in a large pan in the center of the oven on the middle rack. Cook for 1½ hours or until the internal temperature registers 140–150°F (for it to be done medium). Allow the roast to rest at least 20 minutes before slicing. The center should be pinkish-red in color, moist with clear pink juices. After it has rested, slice the lamb into ½-inch thick slices.

To make the lemon-dill Greek yogurt sauce: In a metal bowl, combine all ingredients and store in a container with a lid that has been labeled and dated.

Drizzle the lamb with the yogurt sauce. Orzo goes very well with the lamb.

ORZO WITH FIGS & ONIONS

(SERVES 8)

For the Marrakesh spice mix: (Makes ½ cup)

1 tablespoon ground cumin

1 tablespoon ground ginger

1 tablespoon salt

½ tablespoon ground black pepper

½ tablespoon ground cinnamon

½ tablespoon ground coriander

½ tablespoon turmeric

½ tablespoon cayenne pepper

½ tablespoon ground allspice

1 teaspoon ground cloves

For the orzo:

2 cups orzo pasta

1 pint fresh Mission figs, cut in half lengthwise

6–8 cipollini onions, peeled and cut into quarters

¼ cup fresh lemon juice

¼ cup Marrakesh spice blend

Salt and freshly ground black pepper, to taste

To make the spice mix: Combine all ingredients and store in an airtight container for up to 3 months.

Great for seasoning on all food. Use as dry rub or even as salad dressing base.

To make the orzo: In a medium pot, bring 4 quarts of salted water to a boil. Add the orzo and cook until al dente, about 9 minutes. Strain and set the orzo aside.

Grill the figs, cut side down.

In a hot oiled sauté pan, roast the onions to a golden brown color.

Combine the cooked orzo, grilled figs, roasted onions, lemon juice, and spice blend. Adjust seasoning if needed with salt and freshly ground black pepper.

LOCAL 121

121 WASHINGTON STREET
PROVIDENCE, RI 02903
(401) 274-2121
LOCAL121.COM
EXECUTIVE CHEF TYLER DEMORA

Can't afford a trip to Paris right now? Not to worry. Just make a reservation for dinner at Local 121 in downtown Providence. The moment you step inside this city landmark, you will be immersed in an elegant interior design reminiscent of the "City of Light."

Huge mirrors grace the walls. A black, ivory, and gold color scheme suggests a sophisticated atmosphere. Oversized chairs guarantee a comfortable dining experience. But don't let the refined ambience fool you. This is a modern American restaurant that is

ecologically, culturally, and agriculturally sustainable. Local 121 is aptly named for its commitment to all things local.

The New England clam chowder is made with Matunuck littlenecks. The Point Judith calamari has a chickpea crust. The scallops are Bomster, of course. The burger is made with New England grass-fed beef.

The chef overseeing all this goodness is Tyler Demora, a graduate of the California Culinary Academy in San Francisco, where he worked at the nationally known restaurant Aqua. He also honed his cooking skills at some of the very best restaurants in his native state of Connecticut. Chef Demora's passion for food, especially his use of seasonal ingredients, led him to train with some of the best chefs in Europe before arriving in Providence. Rhode Island is lucky to have him. Make sure you try one of the chef's appetizers: pan-roasted Bomster scallops and squid with sea vegetables, tobiko, and Sauce Nero.

Local 121 is owned by Joshua and Nancy Miller, who opened their restaurant in 2007. The building once housed the Dreyfus Hotel, built in the 1890s, and the Millers have strived to keep much of the original architecture intact. The taproom lounge, also known as The Speakeasy, is not to be missed with its extraordinary stained glass windows. Music is "on tap" there several nights every week.

Smoked Bluefish Pâté

(MAKES 1 PINT OR ENOUGH FOR 4–6 PEOPLE)

8 ounces smoked bluefish

Juice and zest from 1 lemon

12 ounces cream cheese

3 tablespoons heavy cream

3 tablespoons fresh chopped dill

1 teaspoon ground white pepper

3 tablespoons diced shallot

3 tablespoons Worcestershire

1 teaspoon kosher salt

Place all the ingredients into a food processor and pulse until smooth. Serve with your favorite crackers or crostini.

Luxe Burger Bar

5 Memorial Boulevard
Providence, RI 02903
(401) 621-5893
luxeburgerbar.com
Chef de Cuisine Christopher Blouin

Luxe sounds rather posh, but it's really an all-American burger bar and home to the annual build-your-own-burger contest where customers create wildly original burgers. The winning entries are given a spot on the casual restaurant's menu.

Yet another restaurant concept from John Elkhay and his Chow Fun Food Group, Luxe is a popular spot for locals as well as visitors to Providence. It's especially busy on WaterFire nights in the summer when the Providence River is ablaze with a hundred floating bonfires—performance art at its finest.

The interior of Luxe is dark and cool with an eighteen-seat granite-topped bar and an earth-tone decor with touches of red. Huge pop art posters hang on the walls, including an Andy Warhol–type painting of a burger shown in nine different colors.

Chef de Cuisine Christopher Blouin and his team offer an extensive menu loaded with creative, fun food. For starters, they kick calamari up a notch with the addition of buffalo sauce, and they put a new spin on Philly cheesesteaks by turning them into eggrolls. The signature burgers are big and bold. The Death by Burger consists of two Gold Label beef burgers, double amounts of cheddar cheese and smokehouse bacon, smeared with mayonnaise and topped with a fried egg. The Fatty Melt Burger is served between two grilled cheese sandwiches. Truly outrageous, The Frankenstein includes four burgers, two hot dogs, bacon, chili, and coleslaw on buttered rolls with a double order of fries on the side.

According to Chef Blouin, by far the favorite menu item is the build-your-own burger where guests check off everything they want on a special ordering list. They hand their lists to a server, and their custom-designed burgers are delivered to the table. The house-made veggie burger especially gets rave reviews.

Many guests find it impossible to miss out on the famous mac and cheese, which can be custom designed with the addition of bacon, grilled chicken, pastrami, sautéed mushrooms, pulled pork, or broccoli. Three different cheeses are used in this much-loved dish.

Chef Blouin is a dog lover with two of his own at home, so it's no surprise that Luxe is one of several Providence restaurants that offers a doggie menu. Well-behaved dogs and their humans are welcome to dine on the large patio in fair weather. Cocker spaniels, poodles, and mutts lap up mineral water and dine on grilled chicken, burger patties, scrambled eggs, and hot dogs.

Mac & Cheese with Three Cheeses

(SERVES 4)

1½ cups whole milk
1½ cups heavy cream
2 ounces smoked Gouda
2 ounces yellow cheddar cheese
2 ounces Monterey jack cheese
1 pound pasta of your choice (orecchiette is
   recommended)
1 cup chopped raw broccoli
12 bacon strips, cooked and crumbled
Panko bread crumbs, as needed for topping

In a large saucepan, combine the milk and heavy cream over medium heat until simmering. Slowly add the smoked Gouda, and slowly whisk the cheese into the cream mixture. Continue to add all the cheeses slowly until well combined and the sauce is smooth.

In a large pot, cook the pasta according to the directions (al dente is recommended).

Drain the pasta and mix into the cheese sauce mixture. Add the chopped broccoli and bacon, mixing well.

Preheat oven to 350°F.

Pour the pasta mixture into a 9 x 13-inch baking pan, and top with panko bread crumbs. Bake until the top is golden brown, about 25 minutes. If the top is not yet golden brown, place the baking pan under the broiler for just a few minutes more.

New Rivers

7 Steeple Street
Providence, RI 02903
(401) 751-0350
NEWRIVERSRESTAURANT.COM
Executive Chef Beau Vestal

Quite possibly the most romantic restaurant in the city, New Rivers is a little jewel box just waiting for you to discover the beautiful gems inside. Originally, this was a tiny place in a former warehouse, but recent renovations doubled its size. It is still an intimate spot for dinner, either on the bright and airy entrance level or a few steps down into the dark and moody dining room. You can dine on either level. The entrance features a handsome bar, where singles can dine comfortably, with a clear view of the First Baptist Church, dating back to 1638, brilliantly illuminated at night. The lower dining area is well known for its dark green walls, deep red accents, and cozy booths.

Historical preservation is celebrated at New Rivers. The bar was crafted in part from reclaimed lumber. The original wide-plank wood floors were uncovered and refurbished. The façade of the building now mimics the original storefronts of a century ago.

All this is really a playground for Beau and Elizabeth Vestal, the young husband-and-wife team that now owns New Rivers. Beau is the executive chef, and Elizabeth manages the front of the house. This is where they met many years ago when they worked for the former owner, Bruce Tillinghast, one of the original architects of the Providence restaurant landscape. New Rivers opened in 1990, and it was always a very popular restaurant, especially with local residents who became regular customers. Tillinghast sold the business to the Vestals in 2012. The "new" New Rivers seems even more successful than the original.

Chef Vestal's two-page menu offers New American cuisine with global influences, always driven by local and seasonal ingredients. He is a workingman's chef with not a shred of pretense. His close relationships with New England's best farmers and food artisans allow New Rivers to offer handcrafted food with almost everything made from scratch, from the breads and pasta to the cured meats and charcuterie.

For "nibbles and snacks," the menu offers sweet and salty nuts, marinated olives, and a seasonal pickle plate. More substantial starters include roasted tomato bisque, served with to-die-for aged cheddar toasts, and crispy Rhode Island squid (aka calamari) with horseradish and mustard aioli.

A carryover from the early days, the all-natural burger is still on the menu and still served on a Portuguese sweet roll with hand-cut frites. Rhode Island striped bass is

roasted and paired with warm grains. The scallops are grilled and accompanied by succotash. The "Little Chicken" on the menu can be served whole or carved in the kitchen. Depending on the season, it might be served with heirloom tomatoes or root vegetables with cider pan jus.

Another carryover from the early years is the must-have cookie plate dessert, a plate of precious cookies that you will not want to share.

Roasted Tomato Bisque with Aged Cheddar Toasts

(SERVES 4–6)

For the bisque:

5 pounds large red ripe tomatoes
3 tablespoons olive oil, divided
1 head garlic, split horizontally
Salt and black cracked pepper, to taste
2 cups chopped onions
1 tablespoon each dried oregano, basil, and thyme
1 quart vegetable stock (or chicken stock, low sodium)
6 ounces (1½ sticks) cold butter, cubed
1 cup heavy cream

For the cheddar toasts:

4–6 thick slices country loaf (or sourdough)
2 tablespoons extra-virgin olive oil
1 garlic clove
¼ pound aged white cheddar, sliced
Freshly cracked black pepper and olive oil,
    for garnish

To make the bisque: Preheat oven to 400°F.

Toss the tomatoes with some of the olive oil. Add the split garlic head. Season with salt and pepper. Turn the tomato mixture into a large roasting pan, and roast in the oven for 20 minutes, until the tomatoes are nicely colored.

In a large soup pot or stockpot, slowly cook the onions in the remaining olive oil. Add the dry herbs and the roasted tomato mixture. Stew for 5–7 minutes. Add the vegetable stock and simmer for another 25 minutes. Using a blender, blend the soup in batches. Add cubes of butter with each batch. When all the soup is pureed, add the heavy cream and blend well. Season liberally with salt and cracked black pepper.

To make the cheddar toasts: Brush the slices of bread with olive oil, and toast on a sheet tray under the broiler until golden on both sides. Rub the bread slices with garlic. Arrange the cheese slices on each bread slice, and return the sheet tray to the broiler. Cook another 60 seconds, until the cheese has melted.

Serve the tomato bisque in warm soup bowls with the cheese toasts on the side. Add more freshly cracked black pepper to the top of the finished dishes, and drizzle with olive oil.

HERB-ROASTED CHICKEN
WITH ROOT VEGETABLES & CIDER PAN JUS
(SERVES 4)

For the chicken:

1 (3-pound) naturally raised chicken

3 tablespoons unsalted butter, at room temperature

2 garlic cloves

1 tablespoon each dried rosemary leaves, fresh
    parsley leaves, dried thyme leaves

1 lemon, zested and juiced

Salt and pepper, to taste

For the root vegetables:

1 pound each parsnips, carrots, and fennel,
    cut into 2-inch pieces

1 pound baby red potatoes

Olive oil, as needed

Salt and pepper, to taste

For the cider pan jus:

1 cup apple cider
2 cups high-quality chicken broth
1 tablespoon Dijon mustard
1 tablespoon unsalted butter
Salt and pepper, to taste

To make the chicken and root vegetables:
Preheat oven to 350°F.

Truss the chicken with butcher's twine to ensure it cooks evenly. In a food processor, blend the butter, garlic, herbs, lemon zest, and lemon juice into a thick paste. Rub liberally all over the chicken, inside and out. Season the chicken liberally with salt and pepper. Allow to marinate for 30–60 minutes.

In a large bowl, toss the root vegetables and potatoes in olive oil. Season with salt and pepper and arrange in a single layer in a heavy roasting pan. Place the chicken on top of the vegetables.

Roast the chicken and vegetables at 350°F for 40 minutes. Increase the oven temperature to 425°F and roast an additional 6–8 minutes to get the skin golden and crisp. The chicken should register 165°F on a meat thermometer.

Remove the pan from the oven, and transfer the chicken and vegetables to a large sheet tray. Tent with foil to rest and keep warm.

To make the cider pan jus: Remove the fat from the roasting pan, and place the pan on a burner over medium heat. Add the cider and chicken broth, and scrape up any brown bits in the bottom of the pan. Reduce the cider mixture by half. Whisk in the Dijon mustard and butter. Season with salt and pepper.

Carve the chicken into serving pieces, and serve with roasted vegetables, potatoes, and cider jus.

BAKERIES

Bakeries abound in Providence, from the old-fashioned stores you remember from your childhood to the hip, cool, trendy bakeries of today. For a remembrance of things past, LaSalle Bakery and Scialo Bros. will make you feel like a kid again with their colorful fruit tarts, seasonal pies, and Italian cookies. LaSalle Bakery can be found at two locations, 993 Smith Street and 685 Admiral Street. Scialo Bros. Bakery is at 257 Atwells Avenue in the Federal Hill section of the city. Sin at 200 Allens Avenue is wildly creative, while Ellie's at 61 Washington Street transports you to Paris with its French *macarons*.

Just about everyone's favorite is Seven Stars Bakery (401-521-2200), now in three locations in and around Providence. Bakers Jim and Lynn Williams launched Seven Stars in 2001 at 820 Hope Street. I cannot stop in at this bakery/cafe for just a cup of coffee—the gingery gingerbread muffins call my name. And I almost always walk out with a loaf or two of Seven Stars's chewy olive bread, generously studded with oil-cured Moroccan olives and juicy kalamatas. This is serious bread, one that requires a sourdough yeast starter and takes at least 10 days to make. This is artisan bread at its best. Other locations are 342 Broadway in Providence and 20 Newman Avenue in East Providence.

Pane e Vino Ristorante & Enoteca

365 Atwells Avenue
Providence, RI 02903
(401) 223-2230
PANEVINO.NET
Executive Chef Joseph DeQuattro

Ever since Pane e Vino opened in 2002, it has been a local favorite. This Italian restaurant is charming inside and out, with its hanging baskets overflowing with flowers in the summer and then with its red brick fireplace aglow in the winter.

Located on historic Federal Hill, the Little Italy section of Providence, Pane e Vino has a cozy interior with a variety of sections in which to dine. Singles will be comfortable seated at the bar, where dozens of wines are available by the glass. Much in demand are the tables along the front windows with a view of busy Atwells Avenue. Large groups and private parties can be seated in the rear of the restaurant. Every room seems to glow as if the stucco walls were bathed in the Mediterranean sun. The service is equally warm and friendly.

Joseph DeQuattro is the owner and executive chef, overseeing a talented kitchen that produces the southern Italian dishes that Joe grew up on: *antipasto misto,* dry-aged

cured meats, roasted vegetables and artisan cheeses; gnocchi, potato dumplings in a San Marzano tomato sauce; and veal piccata with capers and white wine. A second-generation Italian-American born in Rhode Island, Joe (as he is known to his regular customers) knows his roots as well as what his customers want when it comes to Italian food—fresh, simple and honest.

Pane e Vino, which is Italian for "bread and wine," is not just a restaurant. It is also an *enoteca,* a concept dedicated to giving customers the opportunity to taste a wide variety of wines at reasonable prices. In addition, Pane e Vino offers an impressive gluten-free menu, guaranteeing that everyone in your dinner party will get a true taste of Italy.

Pane e Vino is especially known for its risotto dishes, which change with the seasons. Here it is made with arborio rice, which is available in Italian markets and gourmet shops.

Mushroom Risotto

(SERVES 4–6)

¼ cup extra-virgin olive oil

4 tablespoons butter, divided

1 large white onion, diced

2 cups arborio rice

½ cup dry white wine

8 cups chicken broth, low sodium (you also can use vegetable broth or water)

4 cups chopped mushrooms, your choice

Kosher salt, to taste

1 tablespoon truffle oil (optional)

In a large sauté pan over medium heat, combine the oil and 2 tablespoons of butter. Heat until the butter is melted. Add the onions, and sweat them until the onions are transparent.

Add the rice to the onions. Stir together and toast for a few minutes over the heat, until the rice is well coated and opaque, about 1 minute. Stir in the wine and cook until it is nearly all evaporated. Ladle in the chicken broth, 1 cup at a time, stirring frequently until the rice has absorbed the liquid. The risotto should be slightly firm and creamy, not mushy.

In a separate large sauté pan, melt the remaining 2 tablespoons of butter over medium heat. Add the mushrooms and sauté until golden brown. Be sure not to overcrowd the pan with mushrooms (cook in two batches if needed).

Gently fold the cooked mushrooms into the cooked risotto. Add salt to taste. Drizzle with truffle oil, if desired.

Parkside Rotisserie & Bar

76 South Main Street
Providence, RI 02903
(401) 331-0003
PARKSIDEPROVIDENCE.COM
Executive Chef Antonio DaCosta
Owner Steven Davenport

With a definite Manhattan vibe, Parkside Rotisserie & Bar was opened in 1997 by Steven Davenport, a graduate of the culinary program at Rhode Island School of Design (RISD). As the owner and co-executive chef, Davenport has made Parkside one of the most successful restaurants in Providence with its remarkable food, friendly service, and as they say "location, location, location."

Parkside is at the base of College Hill, where Brown University and RISD coexist. Every year at graduation time, it is virtually impossible to get a reservation at Parkside, which is also located near the Providence River, home to the magical WaterFire performance art event. From May through October, the river is ablaze with a hundred or so small bonfires on selected evenings. Thousands of appreciative people flock to the riverfront on those special nights. Those who are lucky enough to get a table at Parkside are in for an especially memorable night.

Following a serious fire in 2012, Parkside underwent a major renovation. The result is a sophisticated yet casual interior, with works of art by local artists on the walls. This is a comfortable restaurant serving modern-day comfort food, including Parkside's signature rotisserie meat items. Overseeing the open kitchen on a daily basis is the talented Antonio DaCosta, a young chef who comes from a family in the restaurant business. His food is nothing short of dazzling.

The spicy crab cakes are sublime, served with a tomato, corn, and avocado salsa. The Colossal Thai Dumplings are one of those dishes that can never be taken off the menu, with devotees addicted to the savory pillows of goodness served with zesty dipping sauces. The red wine–braised beef short ribs are paired with local root vegetables and roasted garlic mashed potatoes.

But it's the big red rotisserie, imported from France, that steals the show at Parkside. The half chickens are super popular at lunch in a range of flavors: lemon and garlic marinated, spicy lemon and cashew, and herb marinated. At dinnertime, the Peking duck is in big demand, flavored with Chinese five-spice powder, honey, and ginger, and then finished with roasted plum sauce. Simpler grill options include various steaks and chops.

To be succinct, the food at Parkside is innovative, enticing, and upbeat.

CRAB CAKES
WITH AVOCADO CORN SALSA

(SERVES 4)

For the crab cakes:

1 (16-ounce) can jumbo lump crabmeat
1 teaspoon mustard powder
3 tablespoons all-purpose flour
2 tablespoons chopped parsley
1 tablespoon South Shore Shellfish Seasoning
1 egg white
¼ cup mayonnaise
Salt and pepper, to taste
1 cup panko bread crumbs

For the corn salsa:

2 ears freshly shucked corn, with kernels removed
   from cobs
1 Roma tomato, finely diced
½ red onion, finely diced
1 scallion, cut into long, thin strips
¼ cup seasoned rice wine vinegar
1 tablespoon extra-virgin olive oil
Salt and pepper, to taste
1 avocado, shelled and diced

To form the crab cakes: In a large bowl, combine the crabmeat with the mustard powder, flour, chopped parsley, and shellfish seasoning. Using your hands, gently fold in the egg white and mayonnaise until the mixture is moist throughout and well blended. Check for seasoning and adjust as needed with salt and pepper.

Using a 2-ounce ice cream scoop, form the crab cake mixture into small cookie-shaped disks weighing about 2 ounces each. Coat each side of the crab cakes with the panko bread crumbs.

To make the corn salsa: In another bowl, combine the corn, tomato, red onion, and scallion until well mixed. Add the rice wine vinegar, olive oil, salt and pepper, and mix thoroughly. Check for seasoning and adjust as needed. Fold in the avocado last to prevent it from losing the integrity of its texture.

To cook the crab cakes: Preheat oven to 450°F.

In a frying pan on medium-high heat, sear the crab cakes on one side until golden brown. Flip them over and finish cooking in the oven for 6 minutes, or until golden brown and hot in the center.

Place two crab cakes on each plate. Top with the salsa and serve.

MOULES DIJONNAISE

(SERVES 2)

1 tablespoon minced garlic

1 tablespoon minced shallot

Vegetable oil, as needed

2 teaspoons unsalted butter, divided

1 pound fresh mussels

¼ cup white wine

¼ cup heavy cream

2 tablespoons Dijon mustard

1 tablespoon finely chopped tarragon

1 tablespoon finely chopped chervil

Kosher salt and freshly ground black pepper, to taste

In a large frying pan over medium-high heat, sauté the garlic and shallot in a little vegetable oil and 1 teaspoon of unsalted butter. Sauté until the garlic becomes fragrant and nutty, and both the garlic and shallots begin to get some brown color.

Add the mussels to the pan, and stir to get the mussels coated with the sautéed garlic and shallots.

Deglaze the pan with the white wine and let simmer for a minute.

Add the heavy cream and Dijon mustard, and stir until the mussels begin to open and the sauce is well emulsified.

When all the mussels are open, add the chopped herbs. Stir so that the herbs are well incorporated. Season to taste with salt and pepper. Serve the mussels and the sauce in a large bowl with pommes frites or crusty bread for dipping.

RED WINE–BRAISED SHORT RIBS
WITH ROOT VEGETABLES

(SERVES 4)

Vegetable oil, as needed

2 pounds boneless beef short ribs, cut into
    4 (8-ounce) portions

Kosher salt and cracked black pepper, as needed

1 white onion, diced

½ stalk celery, diced

4 parsnips, peeled and diced

2 carrots, peeled and diced

1 tablespoon minced garlic

1 bunch fresh thyme, tied together with butcher's twine

1 bottle red wine

1 tablespoon tomato paste

1 tablespoon red wine vinegar

¼ cup demi-glacé (or if none is available,
    substitute 1 tablespoon beef base)*

*Beef base can be found in the soup aisle of most supermarkets.

Place a rondeau or braising pan on high heat, and coat the bottom of the pan with vegetable oil. Season the short ribs on all sides with salt and pepper.

When the pan starts to smoke, sear the short ribs until they are nicely browned on all sides. This can be done in batches, if necessary. Remove the short ribs from the pan.

Chef DaCosta's note: If done properly, when the short ribs are removed, there should be what is called a "fond" (caramelized proteins from the meat stuck on the bottom of the pan). The pan should be golden and the oil should still be clear without any trace of blackness or burning, which will leave a bitter flavor in the finished product. This may take some controlling of the heat so do not be afraid to adjust the heat during the searing process to prevent this effect.

Add the diced vegetables to the pan and sauté until they start to caramelize. Add the minced garlic and thyme. Deglaze the pan with the red wine. Bring to a simmer and add the tomato paste, vinegar, and demi-glacé. Stir until everything has blended nicely.

Place the short ribs back into the braising pan. They should be almost completely submerged in the liquid.

Preheat oven to 300 °F.

Cover the pan with two layers of foil and place in the oven (a convection oven is recommended, if available). Braise for 3½–4 hours, or until the meat is falling off the bone. (In a conventional oven, this may take another hour or so.)

Remove the short ribs from the braising liquid with a slotted spoon. Be careful so that the short ribs do not fall apart because they should be extremely tender. Strain the sauce and discard the vegetables.

Return the braising liquid to the stove and reduce until it has reached a nappe consistency (coats the back of a metal spoon). Pour the sauce over your short ribs and serve. At Parkside, the red wine–braised short ribs are served with roasted parsnips, baby carrots, and turnips over a side of garlic mashed potatoes.

Rick's Roadhouse

370 Richmond Street
Providence, RI 02903
(401) 272-7675
RICKSROADHOUSERI.COM
Executive Chef Shaun Lampinski

Rick's Roadhouse serves up great big slices of Americana, including authentic barbecue and southern specialties. Imagine, if you will, a cross-country trip down into the delta and then motoring west on Route 66. This is regional American cuisine at its best, with State Fair desserts to die for.

Local restaurateur John Elkhay came up with the concept for Rick's Roadhouse, named after his business partner Rick Bready. It is a vital part of the Chow Fun Food Group, which consists of five totally different restaurants, all in the city of Providence.

On the creative side of the menu, you'll find Texas eggrolls, steak on a stick, and wings from Hell. Guests can create their own burgers from the Burger Bar by selecting what kind of meat they'd like (from beef to bison), and what kind of bun. Then the fun begins, selecting one of five cheeses, six sauces, another three toppings, and side dishes. For the gourmet, there are premium toppings and premium sides to also consider.

Signature sandwiches include a killer fish, a steak bomb, and the ultimate grilled cheese topped with slow-smoked pork from the barbecue pit. Other pit possibilities are Texas beef brisket, baby rack ribs, and sure-to-please combo plates. Health nuts can feast on the blackened salmon salad topped with shrimp and mango salsa. If you somehow have room for dessert, it'll be almost impossible to say no to the Camp Fire S'mores.

Pan-Seared Blackened Salmon Salad with Shrimp & Mango Salsa

(SERVES 4)

4 (6-ounce) salmon fillets, each about 1 inch thick
¼ teaspoon salt
¼ teaspoon black pepper
Cajun seasoning, as needed
1½ cups peeled and cubed mango
¾ cup medium shrimp, cooked and peeled
¼ cup finely chopped red onion
4 teaspoons chopped fresh cilantro
8 teaspoons fresh lime juice, divided
2 teaspoons olive oil

1 fresh jalapeño, seeded and finely chopped
Salt and black pepper, to taste
8 cups mixed salad greens
1 peeled avocado, cut into ¼-inch wedges

Coat a skillet with cooking spray. Place the skillet over medium heat.

Sprinkle the salmon on both sides with salt, pepper, and Cajun seasoning. Pan-sear the salmon for about 4 minutes on each side, turning once.

To make the salsa, combine the mango, shrimp, red onion, cilantro, 4 teaspoons fresh lime juice, olive oil, jalapeño, salt, and pepper.

Combine the salad greens with the remaining fresh lime juice. Season to taste with more salt and pepper.

Arrange about 2 cups of salad greens in the middle of each salad plate. Add the salmon fillet on top of the salad. Top the salmon with about ½ cup of the mango salsa. Garnish each plate with the avocado wedges.

Chicken Fajitas

(SERVES 4)

4 (6-ounce) boneless chicken breasts
Dry rub (equal amounts of paprika, kosher salt, sugar, garlic, chile powder, cumin, black pepper, mustard powder, and cayenne pepper)
1 pound onions, sliced
1 pound green peppers, sliced
6 tablespoons canola oil
12 (6-inch) flour tortillas
12 ounces chopped lettuce
12 ounces sliced cheese, half cheddar and half Monterey jack
1 cup salsa
1 cup sour cream

Coat the chicken breasts on both sides with the dry rub, and place them on a hot grill. Turn the chicken over every few minutes to prevent burning. Grill until the chicken is fully cooked with a slight char on it.

While the chicken is grilling, place the onions, green peppers, canola oil, and 2 teaspoons of dry rub in a 12-inch skillet over medium heat. Cook until the onions and peppers become soft and slightly charred, stirring occasionally.

While both the chicken and vegetables are cooking, place three tortillas and equal amounts of lettuce, the cheese blend, salsa, and sour cream on each plate. When the chicken is fully cooked, slice it into ¼-inch wide pieces.

Place the fully cooked onions and peppers in a hot cast-iron skillet. Top the cooked vegetables with the sliced chicken breasts. Just before serving, add 1 ounce of water to the hot skillet so the vegetables and chicken will sizzle. Serve immediately with the four prepared plates so everyone can make their own fajitas.

BBQ Ribs with Rick's BBQ Sauce

(SERVES 2–4)

For the ribs:

4 pounds pork ribs (approximately 2 full racks)
2 tablespoons light brown sugar
2 teaspoons kosher salt
2 teaspoons paprika
2 tablespoons garlic powder
2 tablespoons onion powder
2 teaspoons cumin
2 teaspoons chile powder
2 teaspoons mustard powder
2 teaspoons cayenne powder
2½ cups Rick's BBQ Sauce (recipe follows)
    or your favorite bottled sauce

For Rick's BBQ Sauce: (Makes about 2½ quarts)

1 quart ketchup
1 quart chile sauce
⅔ tablespoon liquid smoke
⅔ cup cider vinegar
⅔ cup lemon juice
¼ cup Worcestershire sauce
1 cup white sugar
2 cups brown sugar
4 teaspoons each: kosher salt, cumin, chili powder,
    garlic powder, onion powder

To make the ribs: Preheat oven to 325°F.

Peel off the membrane on the underside of the ribs.

Mix together the sugar and all the dry spices to make the dry rub, and apply the rub to the ribs on all sides. Place the ribs on aluminum foil, meat side down, bone side up. Place more foil over the tops of the ribs, and crimp the edges to seal tightly. Place the foiled ribs on a baking sheet, and bake in the oven for approximately 2–2½ hours. The ribs will be done when the meat starts to shrink away from the edges of the bones.

Heat the broiler on low. Arrange the cooked ribs bone side up on a broiler pan, and brush on the BBQ sauce. Broil for 1–3 minutes, watching carefully until the sauce is fully cooked and slightly bubbling. Repeat the same steps for the meat side of the ribs. This step can also be done on a grill, if you prefer.

To make Rick's BBQ Sauce: In a large mixing bowl, mix all the wet ingredients together. In a small mixing bowl, mix all the dry ingredients together. Next combine the wet and dry ingredients until well incorporated.

RUE DE L'ESPOIR

99 HOPE STREET
PROVIDENCE, RI 02906
(401) 751-8890
THERUE.COM
EXECUTIVE CHEF TIM KENNEDY
OWNER DEB NORMAN

It seems as if Rue de l'Espoir has been there forever. In a way that is true because owner Deb Norman is one of those Providence restaurateurs who back in the 1970s helped ignite the city's now-famous restaurant scene. Still charming after all those years, "the Rue" as it's known locally is a very popular American bistro serving breakfast, lunch, and dinner.

This corner restaurant has great curb appeal, especially in the fair weather months. Painted purple and green, the Rue has green awnings to shade its outdoor benches and window boxes that overflow with pretty flowers. Inside, the Rue has two personalities. On one side is a large bar and lounge area; on the other side are comfy booths for dining. Both sections are enveloped in warm earth tones with lots of dark wood, an old-fashioned tin ceiling, and tile-topped tables. A quirky mural covers the walls in the lounge area with eighteen seats at the wood-topped bar. The Rue is a favorite spot for local

college students who often bring their parents in for the award-winning brunch, known especially for its lemon and ricotta cheese griddlecakes.

Executive Chef Tim Kennedy offers an eclectic menu that utilizes local ingredients whenever possible. Some of the small-plate dishes include potato croquettes flavored with cheddar cheese and leeks, a lobster crepe made with Madeira wine, and poutine, a French-Canadian specialty consisting of hand-cut fries topped with cheddar cheese curd, bacon, and gravy. The fig and pistachio salad with feta croutons is a fine start to dinner. Entrees include duck risotto with local corn and a classic bouillabaisse. The Rue is especially known for its huge basket of warm rustic breads brought around to every table as customers dine.

If you like the Rue, you might want to check out its satellite operations, Rue Bis at 95 South Street and Baker Street Rue at 75 Baker Street, both in Providence. Both spots are open for breakfast and lunch.

LEEK & CHEDDAR CROQUETTES WITH HORSERADISH-CHIVE CRÈME FRAÎCHE

(SERVES 4)

For the croquettes:

4 large russet potatoes
2 large leeks
6 ounces clarified butter
1½ cups grated cheddar, loosely packed
Salt and freshly ground black pepper, to taste
1 cup all-purpose flour
2 eggs, beaten
2 tablespoons milk
1 cup panko bread crumbs
Horseradish-chive crème fraîche (recipe follows)

For the horseradish-chive crème fraîche:

½ cup crème fraîche
¼ cup prepared horseradish, drained
2 tablespoons thinly sliced chives
Salt and freshly ground black pepper, to taste

To make the croquettes: Peel the potatoes and cut them into large pieces, reserving them in cold water so they do not oxidize. Drain the potatoes and place them in a large pot. Add cold water to the pot, covering the potatoes completely. Bring the water to a boil. Reduce it to a simmer, and cook the potatoes until fork tender, approximately 20 minutes. Drain the potatoes and set them aside in a large bowl.

Cut the tops off the leeks, and slice the leeks in half lengthwise, then thinly into half moons. Soak the leeks in cold water to release any dirt trapped in the layers. Scoop the leeks out of the water and pat dry.

In a large skillet over medium-high heat, add the clarified butter and sauté the leeks for 5–8 minutes. Pour the leek and butter mixture over the cooked potatoes, and mash well. Fold in the grated cheese. Add the salt and pepper. Refrigerate.

Set up your breading station with plates of flour, egg wash, and panko bread crumbs. To make the egg wash, combine the beaten eggs with the milk.

When the croquette mixture is cool, use a 2-ounce ice cream scoop to portion out small round croquettes. Dredge the croquettes in the flour, cover in egg wash, and bread them with the panko. Place the croquettes on a sheet pan.

These croquettes can be deep fried or shallow fried in a deep skillet. Fry the croquettes until golden brown, and set them on paper towels to drain. Pat the croquettes dry before plating. Place the warm croquettes on a serving plate, allowing two croquettes per person. Top with the crème fraîche. Serve immediately.

To make the horseradish-chive crème fraîche: In a bowl, combine all the ingredients. Set aside.

Grilled Scallops with Corn, Tomatoes & Peas

(SERVES 4)

For the scallops:

12 large sea scallops

Olive oil, as needed

Salt and freshly ground black pepper, to taste

Pea puree (recipe follows)

Corn-tomato sauté (recipe follows)

Fleur de sel (hand-harvested sea salt)

Extra-virgin olive oil, as needed

For the pea puree:

1 shallot, chopped roughly

1 garlic clove, roasted

½ cup roughly chopped celery

2 ounces clarified butter

2 tablespoons white wine

¼ cup cream

½ cup green peas

Salt and freshly ground pepper, to taste

For the corn-tomato sauté:

1 cup fresh corn kernels, cooked

12 cherry tomatoes, sliced in half

Clarified butter, as needed

2 teaspoons fresh thyme

Salt and freshly ground black pepper, to taste

Chef Kennedy's note: These recipes call for clarified butter rather than melted butter. Clarified butter can withstand higher heat. To clarify butter, place two sticks of butter in a heavy saucepan over low heat. Melt the butter slowly. Remove the pan from the stove and let it stand for 5 minutes. Skim the foam from the top. Carefully pour the clarified butter into a container, leaving the milky solids on the bottom of the pan, and cover tightly. Discard the milky solids. Clarified butter will keep in the refrigerator for one month.

To make the pea puree: In a small skillet over medium-high heat, sauté the shallots, garlic, and celery in the clarified butter. Deglaze the pan with the wine, then add the cream. Reduce heat to low. Add the peas and simmer for 5–10 minutes. Puree the mixture in a blender. Pass the pureed peas through a fine strainer. Season to taste with salt and pepper. Set aside.

To make the corn-tomato sauté: In a large skillet over medium-high heat, sauté the corn and tomatoes in the butter. Add the thyme, salt and pepper. Cook for 3–4 minutes. Set aside.

To make the scallops: Preheat the grill.

Make sure you have removed the abductor muscle from each scallop. This is a small, tough muscle on the side of a scallop. Lightly oil and season the scallops. When the grill is hot, place the scallops on the grill, turning them one time on each side to create grill marks and to ensure even cooking. This should take 2–5 minutes, depending on how done you like your scallops.

Spread the pea puree across four serving plates. Add the corn-tomato sauté on top of the puree, and finally the grilled scallops, allowing three scallops per plate. Sprinkle with fleur de sel and drizzle with extra-virgin olive oil. Serve immediately.

Seaplane Diner

307 Allens Avenue
Providence, RI 02905
(401) 941-9547
No website
Chef Mynor "Oscar" Recinos

The all-American diner was born in Providence, Rhode Island, in 1872 when Walter Scott started to sell coffee, sandwiches, and eventually hot food out of a horse-drawn wagon to men working the night shift at the *Providence Journal* newspaper.

That city's most famous diner is Haven Brothers, which opened for business in 1893. Anna Coffey Haven, a widow with eight children, operated the lunch wagon business, which is still in business to this day. Every day around 5 or 6 p.m., the stainless steel trailer is hauled into its regular spot next to City Hall in downtown Providence. It does a brisk business selling burgers and coffee milk until 3 or 4 in the morning, drawing an eclectic crowd of politicians, artists, college students, and every food writer that pays a visit to Providence.

Fast forward to the current millennium, and you'll find Nicks on Broadway, a modern-day diner and one of the city's most popular restaurants serving breakfast, lunch, and dinner. Nicks is at 500 Broadway in the West End of Providence. Owned and operated by the very talented chef Derek Wagner, Nicks on Broadway started out with just eight seats at a tiny counter serving outrageously delicious food. The restaurant and its devoted fan

base have gotten bigger over the years, and you can still find Derek slinging hash (and so much more) there every day.

A classic example of an authentic diner is the Seaplane Diner in South Providence. Produced by the Jerry O'Mahony Diner Company of Elizabeth, New Jersey, in 1953, the Seaplane seats about 60 people in booths and at the counter. Loaded with shiny chrome inside and out, the Seaplane offers classic diner food at very reasonable prices, served by super-friendly waitresses who will surely call you "hon." There's a small Seeburg jukebox at every table. As you enter the Seaplane, make sure you check out the welcoming sign COME IN, WEARY TRAVELER and the small seaplane perched on the roof of the diner.

Mynor "Oscar" Recinos is the "chef" at the Seaplane Diner. Some would argue that he is the head cook there, not a chef, but I beg to differ. Oscar has been at the Seaplane since 1996. Before that, he learned how to cook from some of the city's top restaurant chefs, including Walter Potenza (see page 214). Oscar's family is from Guatemala. An interesting fact: Many of the very best restaurants have Guatemalans working in their kitchens. Oscar is especially known for his Oreo pancakes and made-from-scratch corned beef hash.

CORNED BEEF HASH

(SERVES 6)

2 garlic cloves, minced

4 tablespoons unsalted butter, at room temperature

¼ cup chopped onions

3 cups cooked corned beef, chopped roughly

3 cups cooked peeled potatoes, chopped roughly

Salt, pepper, and parsley, to taste

1 teaspoon garlic powder

1 teaspoon onion powder

¼ teaspoon paprika

In a very large bowl, combine all the ingredients and mix well. Divide equally into six servings. Place each serving on a hot griddle and cover with a heavy weight, such as a bacon press. Cook for 1 minute. Serve immediately as a breakfast side dish.

TEN PRIME STEAK & SUSHI

55 PINE STREET
PROVIDENCE, RI 02903
(401) 453-2333
TENPRIMESTEAKANDSUSHI.COM
EXECUTIVE CHEF LOU CRUZ

On a scale of one to ten, this restaurant definitely is a ten—Ten Prime Steak and Sushi, that is. For more than a decade, Ten has been a popular watering hole for the city's movers and shakers. The award-winning restaurant is known for its designer sushi and aged steaks, prepared skillfully by Executive Chef Lou Cruz.

Ten is yet another jewel in the crown of the Chow Fun Food Group headed by John Elkhay. Starting in the 1980s, Elkhay and a handful of other local chefs helped make Providence a dining destination, so much so that *Travel + Leisure* magazine declared it the number-one food city in the nation in 2013.

With an unmistakable sexy vibe, Ten has a somewhat outrageous wine list with white wines such as Kendall Jackson chardonnay categorized as a blonde, and Silver Oak cabernet listed under redheads. The dinner menu offers steaks and chops with decadent sauces such as horseradish aioli and brandy cream. Ten's famous bacon-wrapped meat loaf is served with cheddar and bacon smashed potatoes and onion strings. Desserts are equally memorable, from the cotton candy crème brûlée to the enormous slice of wedding cake that feeds four to six.

Ten is a visually stimulating restaurant with its undulating bar and touches of cobalt blue. Located in the heart of Providence near the theater district, it's not surprising to spot celebrities dining there.

BACON-WRAPPED MEAT LOAF

(8 SERVINGS PER LOAF)

5 pounds prime ground beef
½ large Spanish onion, minced
1 heaping tablespoon minced garlic
¼ cup ketchup
¼ cup sour cream
½ cup shredded white cheddar cheese
1 cup grated Parmesan cheese
3 large eggs
¼ cup milk
2 tablespoons Worcestershire sauce
3 cups panko bread crumbs or white bread cubes, with the crusts removed

To taste:

Salt
Black pepper
Dried or fresh oregano
Garlic powder
Onion powder

12 slices smoked bacon

Bring the ground beef to room temperature in a large mixing bowl. Preheat oven to 350°F.

In a large sauté pan, sweat the onions and garlic until translucent. Add the onion and garlic mixture to the ground beef. Add all the other ingredients except the bacon to the ground beef mixture. Add seasonings to taste.

Divide the meat loaf mixture equally in 2 (5 x 9-inch) loaf pans just to form the shape of the meat loaf. Remove the meat loaf from each loaf pan. Wrap each loaf with slightly overlapping strips of bacon. Then carefully return each meat loaf to its loaf pan.

Bake for about 1 hour or until the internal temperature reaches 160°F. Pour off any excess fat from each baking pan and allow the meat loaves to cool slightly. Cut each loaf into eight pieces.

TRATTORIA ZOOMA

245 ATWELLS AVENUE
PROVIDENCE, RI 02903
(401) 383-2002
TRATTORIAZOOMA.COM
EXECUTIVE CHEF MARCELLO FLORIO
PIZZAIOLO ALLESANDRO MASTROIANNI

"Zooma, zooma"—so goes the lively refrain in the 1944 classic big band tune "Angelina" by Louis Prima. It's that kind of high-energy fun that can be found at Trattoria Zooma in the Federal Hill section of Providence, the Little Italy of Rhode Island. Add to that a vibrant color scheme and plenty of truly delicious Italian food, and you have a recipe for success.

Don't be surprised if you overhear General Manager Armando Bisceglia speaking in Italian to Executive Chef Marcello Florio, who also converses in Italian with the pizza chef, a true *pizzaiolo*, Allesandro Mastroianni. This talented triumvirate were all born in Italy, and they call Naples their hometown. That's a good sign that the food here is authentic, especially the Neapolitan pizza that's baked in a hand-built wood-fired oven that reaches a temperature of 800°F. Amazing pizzas, such as the Tre Gusti, are created in less than two minutes at Zooma. The Nutella pizza makes for a fine dessert.

Traditional southern Italian cuisine is offered on the menu with many of the pasta dishes made from scratch in the *pastificio*—a small room on the left as you enter, where pasta dough is turned into various cuts including the trattoria's famous gnocchi and ravioli. One of the stars of the menu is the chitarra-style pasta (think thin strands, like guitar strings) flavored with imported speck (very lean Italian bacon) and fresh mushrooms in a rich cream sauce. Whenever possible, vegetables and herbs come from the restaurant's rooftop garden or local farms. The chicken is from Antonelli's Poultry just up the street, and the seafood comes from local fishermen. House specialties include pan-seared sea scallops with crispy polenta and the classic veal Marsala with rosemary roasted potatoes.

A wine list to match all this satisfying fare features wines from all regions of Italy as well as California and Argentina. Zooma also has a state-of-the-art wine dispensing system, which allows patrons to sample high-end wines by the glass.

Inside and out, Zooma is a delight to the eye, from the pinkish-purple on its exterior to the bold turquoise and magenta colors inside. Original works of art are on every wall, many of them from the personal collection of owner Dr. James Cardi. No matter what season it is, Zooma aims to please—with two fireplaces for chilly nights and alfresco dining under sunny skies. Just more ingredients in that recipe for success.

PAGLIA & FIENO, SPECK & FUNGHI

(SERVES 4)

Chef Florio's note: This particular style of pasta can be purchased at Zooma, or you can substitute spaghetti for the chitarra. Chitarra is a fresh egg pasta from the Abruzzo region of Italy. The dough is cut into thin strands on a stringed implement called a *chitarra*, which means "guitar" in Italian.

2 sticks butter

½ cup chopped shallots

1½ cups sliced fresh mushrooms

½ pound San Daniele imported speck, chopped and divided

½ cup white wine

1¾ cups heavy cream

½ pound fontina cheese, grated

1 pound Zooma's fresh chitarra-style Paglia & Fieno, cooked al dente

In a medium frying pan, melt the butter and caramelize the shallots. Add the mushrooms and half of the speck. Add the wine and heavy cream, and reduce until it thickens, which will take about 20 minutes. Mix in the grated cheese and the cooked pasta. Finish by adding some of the remaining raw speck on top of each serving.

Tre Gusti Pizza Napoletano

(MAKES 1 PIZZA, ENOUGH TO SERVE 2)

8 ounces Zooma pizza dough (made with Caputo flour)

3 ounces San Marzano tomato pizza sauce

4 ounces fresh fior di latte mozzarella

2 ounces ricotta

1 ounce diced salami

1 ounce Grana Padano, shaved

2 ounces fresh arugula

Preheat oven to 450°F.

With a rolling pin, flatten the dough into an oval shape. Spread the sauce over ⅔ of the oval. Top the entire oval with the mozzarella cheese. Add the ricotta and salami. Bake in the 450°F oven for 15–17 minutes.

When cooked, add the Grana Padano and fresh arugula to the side of the baked pizza with no sauce.

In *Travel + Leisure*'s America's Favorite Cities poll for 2013, Providence was voted the number-one US city when it comes to the best pizza, beating out Chicago and New York City.

Those major cities certainly have more pizzerias than Providence, but we're talking quality, not quantity, here. For one thing, grilled pizza was created in Providence, at Al Forno specifically, not on the West Coast as some celebrity chefs would have you think. George Germon and Johanne Killeen, chef-owners of the famed Al Forno, grilled their first pizzas in the early 1980s over charwood fires. Grilled pizza remains an essential part of their menu, and having Al Forno's amazing pizza is on every foodie's bucket list.

In more recent times, authentic Neapolitan pizza has become all the rage in Providence. Special pizza ovens, capable of extremely high heat, are being installed in recently renovated restaurants such as Basta in Cranston and Venda Ravioli on Federal Hill in Providence. New pizza joints are popping up here and there, including Providence Coal-Fired Pizza and Figidini's, both in downtown Providence.

For home cooks interested in making their own grilled pizza, there are several options available. You can learn how to make your own pizza dough from scratch, with all the intricacies required when grilled pizza is the goal. Or you can purchase premade pizza crusts or shells, add your own toppings, and then bake or grill the pizza of your dreams. One of the best pizza shells on the market is Top This! fire-grilled pizza, created by Roger Dwyer of Portsmouth, Rhode Island. For years, Dwyer was a "front-of-the-house" instructor at Johnson & Wales University, College of Culinary Arts, and a restaurant consultant. Now retired from teaching, Dwyer devotes his time to his booming pizza crust business.

Top This! pizza crusts are already grilled. Dwyer recommends topping the crusts lightly with quality ingredients, then baking the crusts in an oven or grilling them on an outdoor grill. His website, topthispizzacrusts.com, offers dozens of recipes including Dwyer's own creation topped with pesto, pizza cheese, feta, caramelized onions, chopped tomato pulp, and chopped scallions. This line of premade pizza crusts, as well as other fine brands, is available in all major supermarkets and gourmet shops in Rhode Island.

WATERMAN GRILLE

4 RICHMOND SQUARE
PROVIDENCE, RI 02906
(401) 521-9229
WATERMANGRILLE.COM
EXECUTIVE CHEF TIM MCGRATH

One of the very few waterfront restaurants in Providence, the Waterman Grille is housed in a charming old brick building that used to be a gatehouse overlooking the Seekonk River. In nice weather, diners can watch local college scullers racing on the river.

Part of the well-respected Newport Restaurant Group, Waterman Grille offers three levels of dining with an outdoor deck that wraps around the main floor. That deck has a unique glass railing that fools the eye—you really think there's nothing there to prevent you from falling into the water, but rest assured, everyone on the deck is safely seated.

You can't help but feel romantic when dining at this destination restaurant with its warm ambience, mesmerizing fireplace, and stylish appointments. Through an arched window, diners can see into the semi-open kitchen with its wood-burning grill in constant use. Executive Chef Tim McGrath is the man in charge, delivering creative cuisine made with local products whenever possible. The menu proudly lists local farms and purveyors.

Waterman Grille has been part of the local restaurant scene for more than a decade, but its menu is very forward-thinking. Plates to share include fish tacos, wood-fired pizza, harissa meatballs, wild mushroom spring rolls, and crispy pork belly with pickled radish and candied orange. Out-of-the-ordinary dishes range from a shrimp and smoked

Gouda chowder to a grilled cheese sandwich containing lobster. One of the seafood specialties is the pan-roasted local fluke, served with sweet corn soubise and a sauté of swiss chard, Yukon Gold potatoes, and chorizo.

Signature dishes such as the lobster mac and cheese border on the decadent side of life. Short ribs, lamb shanks, and duck are some of the other house specials.

What is it about the Waterman Grille that makes this restaurant so special? Perhaps it's the way men seem handsomer and women lovelier than ever when dining there. But it's more the exquisite food and impeccable service that well deserve the credit for Waterman Grille's sterling reputation.

ROASTED SCALLOPS WITH BUTTERNUT SQUASH PUREE, BRUSSELS SPROUT SLAW & PANCETTA VINAIGRETTE

(SERVES 4)

For the butternut squash puree:

½ cup (1 stick) butter
1 cup finely diced sweet onion
1 tablespoon minced garlic
2 cinnamon sticks
1 cup white wine
3 cups chopped butternut squash
3 cups heavy cream
Salt and white pepper, to taste
Lemon juice, to taste

For the pancetta lardons:

½ cup water
6 ounces pancetta, finely diced

For the brussels sprout slaw:

½ pound brussels sprouts, shaved
1 cup julienned carrots
1 cup shredded red cabbage
1 tablespoon canola oil
Salt and white pepper, to taste
½ cup pancetta lardons (see recipe above)
1 teaspoon lemon juice

For the pancetta vinaigrette:

⅛ cup balsamic vinegar
½ garlic clove
1 teaspoon whole-grain mustard
¼ cup warm rendered pancetta fat (reserved from the lardons)
Salt and white pepper, to taste

For the pan-roasted scallops:

16 large sea scallops
Salt and white pepper, to taste
Canola oil, as needed
Local baby greens, for garnish

To make the butternut squash puree: In a saucepan, melt the butter. Add the onions and cook over medium heat until caramelized, about 12 minutes. Add the garlic, cinnamon sticks, and white wine. Cook until all the liquid has evaporated.

Add the butternut squash and heavy cream. Cook over medium-low heat until the squash is fork-tender, about 20 minutes. Remove the cinnamon sticks, and puree the squash mixture in a blender. Strain through a fine-mesh strainer. Season to your liking with salt, white pepper, and lemon juice.

To make the pancetta lardons: In a sauté pan, add the water and pancetta. Cook over medium heat until all the water has evaporated and the pancetta crisps in its own fat, about 15–20 minutes. Strain the lardons. Reserve the rendered fat for the vinaigrette.

To make the brussels sprout slaw: Preheat oven to 400°F.

In a large mixing bowl, combine the brussels sprouts, carrots, cabbage, and canola oil. Season with salt and white pepper. Mix until well combined.

Place the mixture on a sheet tray and bake in a 400°F oven for 5–7 minutes, or until the brussels sprouts are golden brown. Remove the sheet tray from the oven, and transfer the mixture to a large bowl. Add the pancetta lardons and lemon juice. Season with salt and white pepper. Serve warm.

To make the pancetta vinaigrette: In a blender, combine the vinegar, garlic, and whole-grain mustard. Pulse until incorporated. With the blender on low speed, slowly drizzle in the warm pancetta fat. Season with salt and white pepper. Keep at room temperature (if refrigerated, the vinaigrette will separate).

To make the pan-roasted scallops: Season the scallops with salt and white pepper.

Place a sauté pan over high heat. Pour in enough oil to coat the bottom of the pan. When the pan is almost smoking, add the scallops. Do not overcrowd the pan. Lower the heat to medium-low. Cook the scallops for 1–2 minutes on each side until golden brown and a nice crust develops. Remove the scallops from the pan. Do not overcook.

To plate: Place 3–4 ounces of the butternut puree on each plate. Neatly place the brussels sprout slaw on top of the purée. Arrange four scallops on top of the slaw. Spoon 1 ounce of the vinaigrette over the scallops. Garnish with baby greens.

Pan-Roasted Local Fluke
with Sweet Corn Soubise, Sautéed Swiss Chard, Potatoes & Chorizo

(SERVES 4)

For the basil oil:

½ gallon water
1 tablespoon salt
1 teaspoon baking powder
2 bunches basil
Ice water, as needed
½ cup canola oil
¼ teaspoon white pepper
Local baby greens, for garnish

For the sweet corn soubise:

1 stick butter
1 cup chopped sweet onions
2 garlic cloves, chopped
5 cups corn kernels, freshly cut from the cob
3 cups heavy cream
Salt, white pepper, and lemon juice, to taste

For the sauté of swiss chard, potatoes & chorizo:

1 teaspoon canola oil
1 cup medium diced chorizo
2 cups large diced Yukon Gold potatoes, blanched
4 cups swiss chard (stems removed), chopped
1 tablespoon butter
Salt and white pepper, to taste

For the pan-roasted fluke:

Canola oil, as needed
4 (8-ounce) fluke fillets
Salt and white pepper, to taste

To make the basil oil: In a saucepan, bring the water to a boil. Add the salt and baking powder (baking powder will keep the basil a vibrant green). Dip the basil in the boiling water for 2–3 seconds (no longer, or the basil will turn black). Take the basil directly from the boiling water into the ice water to shock and immediately stop the cooking process. Remove the basil from the ice water. Allow the basil to come to room temperature. Pat dry with a paper towel.

Add the oil, basil, and white pepper to a blender. Blend 2–3 minutes until smooth. Place in an airtight container in the refrigerator overnight. The solids will settle at the bottom, and the basil oil will float on top. Decant the oil from the top, making sure you do not disturb the solids on the bottom. Discard the solids and reserve the oil.

To make the sweet corn soubise: In a saucepan, melt the butter over medium heat. Add the onions and garlic. Sweat over medium low-heat until translucent (do not caramelize). Add the corn and cream. Cook over medium heat for about 20 minutes, or until the cream has reduced by a quarter. Puree the mixture in a blender until smooth, and strain through a fine-mesh strainer. Season with salt, white pepper, and lemon juice.

To make the sauté of swiss chard, potatoes & chorizo: In a large sauté pan, heat the oil. When hot, add the chorizo. Cook until crisp. Add the blanched potatoes. Sauté until the potatoes have a golden brown color and are crisp. Add the swiss chard and cook 2–3 minutes until tender. Add the butter, and season with salt and white pepper.

To make the fluke: In a sauté pan over high heat, add 1–2 tablespoons of oil. Just before the pan starts to smoke, place the fish presentation side down in the pan. (Fluke is usually skinless.) Lower the heat to medium-low. Cook 3–4 minutes over medium-low heat until the fish is golden brown and has a nice crust. Turn the fish over, and remove from the heat. Allow the fish to rest in the pan 30–40 seconds, or until the fish is cooked through. Remove the fish from the pan, and let rest 1 minute. Season to taste with salt and white pepper.

To plate: Place ½ cup of the corn soubise in the center of each plate. Neatly place the swiss chard mixture on top of the corn soubise. Place the pan-roasted fluke on top of the swiss chard sauté. Garnish with basil oil and local baby greens.

XO Cafe

125 North Main Street
Providence, RI 02903
(401) 273-9090
XOCAFE.COM
Executive Chef Marty Lyons

XO . . . what does it stand for? Extraordinary? Or simply kisses and hugs? You be the judge after visiting this city restaurant that's been winning accolades since 1997 when it opened under the direction of John Elkhay, chef turned restaurateur and the creative genius in charge of the Chow Fun Food Group.

One of the most romantic restaurants in the city, XO Cafe has a well-deserved reputation for outstanding food. That image increased tenfold when Marty Lyons came on board as the executive chef. A veteran of the local food scene, Lyons paid his culinary dues at several of the very best restaurants in Providence. His farm-to-table menu is beyond tempting: roasted free-range chicken from Baffoni's Poultry Farm in nearby Johnston, seared Bomster scallops, and potato-wrapped Atlantic halibut.

The formally set restaurant is especially known for its grilled steaks—pure Hereford beef aged for at least 28 days—offered with red wine demi-glacé, blue cheese au poivre, chimichurri, or tamarind steak sauce. The side dishes are just as tempting, especially the bacon mac and cheese, garlic Yukon Gold mashed potatoes, and Parmesan truffle fries with rosemary aioli.

XO Cafe is one of those clever restaurants that suggest you should order dessert first since life is so short. A summer favorite is the strawberry-rhubarb crisp with vanilla

custard ice cream. The molten chocolate cake with raspberry sorbet is always on the menu.

Housed in the historic (1799) John Updike House, XO Cafe offers candlelit dining as well as a lively cocktail scene at the bar. Works of art on the walls help create the seductive atmosphere. Special events are always playful in nature. If you go to the Sunday brunch in your pajamas, you get a complimentary mimosa or Bloody Mary.

Crispy Chicken Confit
with Sautéed Kale, Cauliflower Puree & Carrot-Citrus Gastrique

(SERVES 4)

For the chicken/cure:

1 teaspoon black peppercorns
½ teaspoon fennel seed
½ teaspoon allspice berries
½ teaspoon juniper berries
¼ teaspoon red pepper flakes
3 sprigs fresh thyme, roughly chopped
½ cup kosher salt
½ cup brown sugar
2 garlic cloves, minced
Zest of 1 orange
4 chicken leg quarters
6 cups duck fat (can substitute olive oil)

For the cauliflower puree:

Olive oil, as needed to coat the bottom of a pan
1 medium yellow onion, peeled and diced
3 garlic cloves, minced
¼ cup white wine
1 head cauliflower, cored and roughly chopped
1 pint heavy cream
3 tablespoons unsalted butter
Juice of ½ lemon
Salt and pepper, as needed

For the carrot-citrus gastrique:

½ cup sugar
1 cup carrot juice (store-bought, or the juice of approximately 3 large carrots if you have a juicer)
½ cup white vinegar
Juice of 1 orange
Juice of 1 lemon
Salt and pepper, as needed

For the sautéed kale:

2 tablespoons olive oil
3 garlic cloves, minced
Pinch red pepper flakes
1 large bunch curly kale, stripped from the stems and cut into ½-inch ribbons
¼ cup white wine
Salt and pepper, as needed

To cure the chicken: In a small bowl, combine the peppercorns, fennel, allspice, juniper, red pepper flakes, and thyme. Transfer the spices to a mortar and pestle, and lightly crush. You can also pour the spices onto a cutting board and use the back of a sauté pan to crush them if you do not have a mortar and pestle.

Combine the spice mixture with the salt, sugar, garlic, and orange zest. Sprinkle the mixture all over the chicken, and place the chicken in a deep casserole. Cover and refrigerate overnight.

To make the chicken confit: Preheat oven to 275°F.

Remove the chicken legs from the cure, rinse thoroughly, and pat dry with a paper towel. Pack the chicken legs tightly in a small deep roasting pan, and cover completely with duck fat or olive oil. Cook the legs in the oven for 2–2½ hours, leaving the pan open, until they are easily pierced with the tip of a knife.

Carefully remove the legs from the hot oil, and transfer them to a cooling rack set over a baking sheet. Let drain for 20 minutes. Reserve the confit oil.

To make the cauliflower puree: Place a heavy-bottomed saucepan over medium heat. Add the olive oil, and lightly sauté the onions and garlic without letting them brown. Deglaze the pan with white wine, and cook down for 2 minutes. Add the cauliflower and cream. Bring to a boil and then reduce to a simmer while stirring occasionally. After 10–15 minutes, the cauliflower should be tender.

Combine the cauliflower mixture, butter, and lemon juice in a blender. Puree until smooth. Make sure to start the blender off on a slow speed to avoid having the hot liquid spray out the top. Adjust to taste with salt and pepper. Transfer to a small pot, cover, and keep warm until serving time.

To make the gastrique: In a small saucepan, combine the sugar and carrot juice. Heat the mixture over medium-high heat until the sugar dissolves and begins to bubble. Reduce the mixture until it begins to caramelize. It should turn a light golden color. Once the mixture is caramelized, add the vinegar. The sugar will harden at first, and then dissolve again when it comes back to a boil. Once the sugar has re-dissolved, add the orange juice and lemon juice. Continue to cook the gastrique until it is reduced and thickens a little. Season with salt and freshly cracked pepper. Set aside and keep warm.

To sauté the kale: Heat the olive oil in a large sauté pan over high heat. Add the garlic and pepper flakes, and allow to bloom in the oil for a few seconds. Add the kale and sauté over high heat for 30–40 seconds. Add the wine to the pan, toss several times, and let the kale wilt down.

Remove the pan from the heat, and season with salt and pepper. Keep warm until it is time to serve.

To plate the dish: Preheat oven to 400°F.

Heat an oven-safe sauté pan over medium heat. Add a few tablespoons of the confit oil, and place the chicken legs skin side down in the pan. Place the pan in the oven for 8–10 minutes.

Spoon the cauliflower puree onto the center of each plate. Top with the sautéed kale.

When the skin is golden brown and crispy, remove the chicken legs from the oven and place on top of the kale. Drizzle the gastrique around the plate and over the chicken. Serve immediately.

NEWPORT

Castle Hill Inn

590 Ocean Drive
Newport, RI 02840
(401) 849-3800
CASTLEHILLINN.COM
Executive Chef Karsten Hart

There are so many options awaiting you at the Castle Hill Inn, without a doubt one of the finest restaurants in Newport. Established in 1875, this Relais & Chateaux property sits on forty waterfront acres with elegant rooms and cottages on the beach for overnight guests.

To lunch at Castle Hill is a divine experience. The lobster velouté is kissed with tarragon crème fraîche. The simple-sounding mixed green salad is actually complex with Earl Grey pickled beets, Vermont goat cheese, and tarragon-buttermilk dressing. The artisanal cheese tasting also offers fruit jam, Marcona almonds, Aquidneck Island honey, and grilled bread. Three cheeses and roasted tomato marmalade are used in the grilled cheese sandwich with creamy onion soup on the side.

Dinner is exquisite with three degustation menus to consider: three courses, five courses, and eight courses, all with recommended wine pairings. Just some of the possibilities are pan-seared Hudson Valley foie gras, butter-poached Maine lobster, grilled filet of Hereford beef, grilled native swordfish, pan-roasted halibut, and roasted duck breast, with each entree sporting simply amazing accompaniments. A vegetarian menu is also available. Dinner is served in the aptly named Sunset Room. This is fine dining at its finest with remarkable service to match.

But Sunday brunch with live jazz just might be Castle Hill at its best. The basic brunch menu includes Matunuck oysters on the half shell, a pretzel bagel with house-smoked salmon, a ridiculously delicious lobster roll, and Maine lobster hash. New England clam chowder is served with a black pepper–thyme biscuit. Classic brunch dishes are also available, from eggs Benedict to brioche french toast with chantilly cream.

Castle Hill has four dining rooms, but the hottest ticket (at least from Memorial Day in May to Columbus Day in October) is dining on the tiered bluestone terrace or sitting in Adirondack chairs on the lawn. Out on the gently sloping lawn, with a panoramic view of Narragansett Bay alive with pleasure craft, a substantial "small plate" menu is offered for easy dining while relaxing in the classic white chairs. Raw bar items with a glass of Champagne are common fare as well

as creative salads, appetizers, and sandwiches. Entrees on the lawn include native fluke, lobster, and *steak-frites*. The outdoor bar is heated so you'll find hearty souls out there until November.

All this marvelous food is brought to you by Executive Chef Karsten Hart and his talented culinary team. Born in Louisiana to German and Sicilian parents, Chef Hart is a mélange of culinary influences. He spent ten years in northern California honing his skills at a Relais & Chateaux property. When Chef Hart arrived in Newport in 2010, he said: "I was the proverbial kid in a candy store, amazed by Rhode Island's local farms and fishermen." When approaching a dish, he always hopes to find creative ways to work with local ingredients.

PORK & CLAMS WITH LITTLENECK STUFFIES, DILL-BUTTER CLAM BROTH & GRILLED BROCCOLI RABE

(SERVES 2)

For the pork:

2 pork tenderloins
1 teaspoon extra-virgin olive oil
Salt and freshly ground pepper, to taste
1 tablespoon chopped thyme
½ tablespoon oregano

For the littleneck stuffies:

12 fresh littleneck clams, alive and still in their shells
Reserved clam liquor
1 tablespoon butter
1 tablespoon ground bacon
1 cup sliced oyster mushrooms
1 shallot, minced
1 garlic clove, minced
2 celery ribs with leaves removed, minced
1 green bell pepper, cored, seeded, and finely diced
Salt and freshly ground black pepper, to taste
1 bunch spinach leaves, washed
¼ cup dry white wine
½ cup heavy cream

1 tablespoon chopped parsley
Tabasco, to taste
Worcestershire sauce, to taste

For the dill-butter clam broth:

2 tablespoons butter
2 tablespoons ground bacon
2 shallots, diced small
1 celery stalk, diced small
1 garlic clove, minced
1 teaspoon all-purpose flour
2 quarts fresh clam juice
2 cups heavy cream
2 teaspoons chopped dill
Salt, pepper, lemon juice, Tabasco, and
    Worcestershire sauce, to taste

For the grilled broccoli rabe:

1 pound broccoli rabe, stems removed
3 tablespoons extra-virgin olive oil
Salt and freshly ground black pepper, to taste

To make the pork: Using a sharp butcher's knife, begin by removing any excess fat from the pork tenderloins. Rub the oil over the tenderloins to coat lightly. Carefully remove any silver skin. Season the tenderloins with salt, pepper, and fresh herbs. Wrap each tenderloin with plastic wrap, then with aluminum foil to create a uniform roll, also known as a roulade.

Fill a 6-quart pot $2/3$ full of water. Bring the water to a boil, then reduce heat to a simmer. Place the roulades in the simmering water, checking the temperature after 8 minutes with an instant-read meat thermometer. This is usually not enough time for the pork to be fully cooked, but a good point to see what the internal temperature is (it should be about 90°F). Place the pork back in water for an additional 2–4 minutes. This will raise the temperature to 130°F. Allow the pork to rest until the internal temperature reaches 142°F. Remove the pork from the plastic/aluminum foil wrapping, and slice into 6 medallions.

To prepare the littleneck clams: Begin by scrubbing the clams with a brush under cold running water. Fresh, live clams should always feel heavy for their size (due to their full state of hydration), and they should be tightly closed.

Shuck the clams with a clam knife, taking care to leave the clam meat inside each shell. Reserve all the clam liquor. Remove any excess shell particles from each clam, and leave the clam in the bottom of each shell, ensuring that it has been separated from the shell.

To prepare the filling for the stuffies, melt the butter in a medium heavy-bottomed pot over low heat. Add the bacon, and cook until the bacon fat has been rendered. Turn up the heat, and add the mushrooms. Sauté until they just start to lightly brown. Add the shallot, garlic, celery,

and bell pepper. Sauté for another minute or until vegetables are soft. Season the mixture with salt and freshly ground black pepper. Add the spinach, clam liquor, white wine, heavy cream, and parsley. Reduce this liquid mixture by half. Season to taste with Tabasco, Worcestershire sauce, salt and pepper. Remove from the heat and let cool.

Preheat oven to 350°F.

Using a teaspoon, stuff each clamshell with the filling. Place the stuffed shells on a baking sheet. Bake at 350°F for 4 minutes or until golden brown. Remove the baking sheet from the oven, and reserve for plating.

To prepare the clam-dill sauce: Melt the butter in a large pot over medium heat. Add the bacon and cook for 5–7 minutes. Add the shallots, celery, and garlic, and cook for 3 minutes or until tender. Add the flour and cook for an additional 3 minutes, stirring constantly with a wooden spoon to keep the flour from sticking to the bottom of the pan. Add the clam juice and heavy cream, and simmer for 20 minutes. The liquid should thicken just slightly. Add the fresh dill, and season to taste with salt, pepper, lemon juice, Tabasco and Worcestershire sauce.

To make the broccoli rabe: In a large stainless steel bowl, combine all ingredients and mix thoroughly. Place the seasoned broccoli rabe on a hot grill and cook until wilted. Adjust seasoning and reserve for plating.

To plate the dish: Preheat two large entree bowls. Place the grilled broccoli rabe in the center of each bowl. Arrange six pork medallions and six stuffies around the grilled greens. Pour 3 ounces of the clam broth into each bowl. Serve with a crispy baguette and a cold beer.

Clarke Cooke House

BANNISTER'S WHARF
NEWPORT, RI 02840
(401) 849-2900
CLARKECOOKE.COM
EXECUTIVE CHEF TED GIDLEY

For many Rhode Islanders, the Clarke Cooke House holds dear memories. It seems like it's been there forever on Bannister's Wharf in the very heart of Newport's waterfront. In reality, the Clarke Cooke House opened its doors as a restaurant in 1973, and over the next four decades it's been the site of many a first date, many a wedding, and many a special anniversary.

And this historic restaurant also has many an area for dining and dancing with no less than seven distinct rooms on three different levels in the eighteenth-century building. The Porch with wicker furniture offers romantic dining while the Candy Store is more casual with its slouchy deck chairs. Cocktails are offered at the Sky Bar and Midway Bar with spectacular sunset views. Filled with yachting memorabilia, the Club Room is open year-round. In warm weather, the Bistro opens all its windows to the sights and sounds of busy Bannister's Wharf. And who can resist checking out the Boom Boom Room with its high-energy dance floor?

What's new at the Clarke Cooke House? A spectacular raw bar is the first thing you spot upon entering the building, and cutting-edge sushi has been added to the summer menu.

There is so much to see within the Clarke Cooke House. The centuries-old floors creak, and at times you almost feel as if you are on board an old sailing ship. A very dark green is the signature color, from the walls of an upper-level dining area to the official dinner plates inscribed with the name of this venerable restaurant.

All in all, the Clarke Cooke House sounds like a fun spot, but on its serious side you'll find the imaginative food of Executive Chef Ted Gidley. Nothing but the freshest seafood, the finest beef, and the best regional produce will do for this master chef. This is fine dining at its finest with the main menu offering foie gras, squab, and Kobe beef as appetizers. Rhode Island's historic johnnycakes are given a modern-day twist when Chef

Gidley tops them with smoked salmon, crème fraîche, and caviar. For the main course, entrees include wood-grilled swordfish, rack of lamb, and prime New York sirloin steak au poivre. That swordfish is a summer-only dish, when the local waters are teeming with that particular species.

The varied menu changes with the seasons. Come fall, the open-air restaurant closes its many windows and lights an all-night fire in its massive fireplace. Unlike some Newport restaurants, the Clarke Cooke House is open year-round, much to the delight of locals and off-season tourists.

Rhode Island Johnnycakes with Smoked Salmon, Crème Fraîche & Caviar

(SERVES 4)

Chef Gidley's note: This johnnycake recipe is a variation and was inspired by Jasper White's *Cooking from New England*.

For the johnnycake batter:

1 cup milk

1 cup Kenyon's stone ground cornmeal

1 egg

1 pinch kosher salt

2–3 teaspoons butter, per serving

For the crème fraîche:

2 ounces crème fraîche, whipped into soft peaks

2 teaspoons sherry vinegar

2 teaspoons pure maple syrup

2 teaspoons fresh dill, washed, picked, and chopped fine

For serving:

Thinly sliced smoked salmon, rolled into rosettes, 2 per serving

½ teaspoon American sturgeon caviar, 2 per serving

1 teaspoon diced red bell pepper (¼-inch dice), per serving

1 teaspoon diced yellow bell pepper (¼-inch dice), per serving

2 dill sprigs, washed and cleaned, per serving

In a bowl, whisk all the batter ingredients together, except the butter, and reserve.

In another bowl, whisk all the crème fraîche ingredients together and reserve.

Heat a crepe pan over moderately high heat. When the pan is hot, add the butter. As soon as it melts, pour 2 tablespoons of johnnycake batter in perfect circles. Allow to cook for about 45 seconds, then flip with a spatula, and cook for about 15 seconds more. The johnnycakes should be crisp and well browned. Place them quickly on a paper towel to absorb excess butter.

Place two johnnycakes side by side on each plate. Top each johnnycake with a salmon rosette, 1 teaspoon of the crème fraîche mixture, and about ½ teaspoon of caviar.

Garnish on either side with the diced peppers and dill sprigs.

Native Heirloom Tomato Salad

(SERVES 4)

Chef Gidley's note: With the exception of the dressing, most of this recipe is approximate and can be scaled in any way you prefer. The heirloom tomatoes at the Clarke Cooke House are supplied by Greenview Farm in Wakefield, Rhode Island.

For the tomato salad:

2 pounds heirloom tomatoes, as many different varieties
 as possible: Black Krim, Brandywine, Green Zebra,
 Cherokee Purple, Prudence Pride, Rose, Dad's
 Sunset, Persimmon, and Gold Medal (Pineapple),
 to name a few
Sea salt, to taste
1 English cucumber, washed, peeled, and cut into
 ⅓-inch slices
½ cup cooked corn kernels
½ cup chèvre (goat cheese), crumbled
2 tablespoons toasted pine nuts
1 tablespoon chiffonade of fresh basil (cut into strips
 about ¼-inch wide)

For the balsamic vinaigrette:

3 cups finest quality extra-virgin olive oil
1 cup finest quality aged balsamic vinegar
Pinch of kosher salt

For the basil oil:

1 cup fresh basil leaves, blanched and chilled in
 an ice bath, then strained
2 ounces extra-virgin olive oil

To make the balsamic vinaigrette: Place the vinaigrette ingredients in a blender. Blend, then reserve.

To make the basil oil: Combine the strained basil leaves with the extra-virgin olive oil. If available, place this basil oil in a squirt bottle for garnishing each finished salad plate.

To serve: Wash and core all the tomatoes. Cut the tomatoes into ½-inch slices. On each salad plate, place a variety of the sliced heirloom tomatoes in a circular pattern overlapping one another. Season the tomatoes with sea salt. Add a layer of the sliced cucumbers and some of the cooked kernels of corn. Dress the salad components with 2 ounces of the balsamic vinaigrette. Use a 2-ounce ladle to do this, and be sure to rotate the dressing vertically before dressing each salad to keep it well blended. (The ingredients easily separate so you need to rotate the ladle in order to get some of the oil blended with some of the vinegar.) Top each serving with some of the crumbled chèvre, pine nuts, and basil. Garnish with a few drops of basil oil around the plate.

Wood-Grilled Swordfish
with Corn Coulis, Hash, Tomato Preserve & Wild Mushrooms

(SERVES 2, CAN BE DOUBLED)

Chef Gidley's note: The best swordfish comes from local waters off Block Island, preferably during the months of July, August, and September. At the Clarke Cooke House, we use a wood-fired grill, and it is easy to control the temperature manually. With gas-fired grills, this is not the case, so I recommend starting the swordfish on the "hot spot" and rotate the steak once to get a grid pattern set of marks, then flip it with a spatula, and move it to a less intense heat until it is medium rare, medium, or whatever the preference may be.

For the corn coulis:

1 leek, white part only, sliced and washed well,
   with all sand removed
¼ cup extra-virgin olive oil
4 cups cooked corn kernels
3 cups chicken stock
Salt and white pepper, to taste
Pinch of nutmeg

For the hash:

2 tablespoons canola oil
1 large all-purpose potato, washed, peeled, and
   cut into ⅓-inch dice
1 tablespoon sliced leeks, white part only, washed well,
   cut into ¼-inch slices on the bias, and chopped
½ cup cooked corn kernels
1 tablespoon cooked bacon (cut into ¼-inch wide strips
   and rendered until crisp, fat reserved)
1 tablespoon finely sliced scallions, green part only
1 tablespoon diced roasted red pepper (¼-inch dice)
1 tablespoon fresh English peas, blanched
Salt and pepper, to taste

For the tomato preserve:

1 cup finely sliced red onions
2 tablespoons extra-virgin olive oil

1 cup tomato confit (see chef's note on page 123),
   cut into ½-inch dice
¼ cup fresh tarragon, washed, picked, and chopped
¼ cup granulated sugar
¼ cup sherry vinegar
Salt and pepper, to taste

For the wild mushrooms:

1 ounce king oyster mushrooms, washed and
   cut into ¼-inch slices
1½ tablespoons extra-virgin olive oil
1 teaspoon finely diced shallots
1 teaspoon minced garlic
Salt and pepper, to taste

For the basil oil:

1 cup fresh basil leaves, blanched and chilled in
   an ice bath, then strained
¼ cup extra-virgin olive oil
Pinch of kosher salt

For the swordfish:

2 (8-ounce) fresh swordfish steaks, about 1 inch thick
Canola oil, as needed
Salt and pepper, to taste

To make the corn coulis: Over moderate heat, sweat the leeks in the olive oil until translucent. Do not allow the leeks to brown. Add the corn and enough chicken stock to cover the corn. Bring the mixture to a boil. Transfer the mixture to a blender, and blend on high speed. Pass the puree through a fine sieve. Season with the salt, pepper, and nutmeg. Keep the coulis hot in a *bain marie* or water bath.

To make the hash: Over moderately high heat, heat the oil and brown the potatoes on all sides until cooked through. Add the leeks and cook until translucent. Add the rest of the ingredients, and cook until hot. Season with salt and pepper, and add some of the reserved bacon fat if desired. Keep hot.

To make the tomato preserve: Sweat the onions in the olive oil until translucent. Do not allow to brown. Add the tomato confit, tarragon, sugar, and vinegar, and bring to a boil. Season with salt and pepper. Keep hot.

Chef Gidley's note: At the Clarke Cooke House, we use tomato confit for this and many other recipes. We first blanch and chill tomatoes, peel them, deseed them, and then roast them on a sheet pan with olive oil, garlic, and thyme in a 350°F oven. For this recipe, simply blanching

ripe tomatoes for 10 seconds, chilling in an ice bath, peeling, deseeding, and dicing would be sufficient. This is known as concassé in the culinary world.

To prepare the wild mushrooms: Over moderately high heat, sauté the mushrooms in the olive oil until browned. Flip them with a spatula. Add the shallots and garlic. Season to taste, and keep hot. It may be necessary to add more oil during the sauté, as mushrooms tend to absorb the oil.

To make the basil oil: Place the basil and oil in a blender. Blend and season with a pinch of kosher salt. Set aside.

To prepare the swordfish: Coat each swordfish steak with canola oil, season with salt and pepper, and grill over high heat to start. See the chef's note on page 122.

For presentation: Place 2 ounces of the corn coulis in the center of each dinner plate. Place a serving of the hash in the center of the coulis, and place the swordfish steak right on top of the hash. Top the swordfish with about 1 ounce of the tomato preserve and 2 or 3 slices of mushrooms. Garnish with the basil oil around the coulis, and serve immediately.

FLUKE WINE BAR & KITCHEN

41 BOWEN'S WHARF
NEWPORT, RI 02840
(401) 849-7778
FLUKEWINEBAR.COM
EXECUTIVE CHEF KEVIN KING

Whatever the season, you're in for a special treat at Fluke—in terms of the view as well as the food. Seated in the main dining room of Fluke, you almost feel like you're in a stylish tree house with a sunset view of Newport Harbor. When autumn arrives, the busy tourist season slows down, and leaves fall from nearby trees, providing dinner guests with an

even broader view of the waterfront. In winter, there's nothing prettier than a light snowfall seen through the second-floor windows. In springtime, you can almost witness the buds on the branches bursting open, which then brings us back to Newport's high season of summer.

Executive Chef Kevin King's food is just as seasonal. His creative menu changes almost daily, depending on what's perfectly ripe and fresh. Hailing from Manhattan, where he worked with several acclaimed chefs, King has a strong background in French, Italian, and Asian cuisines. He creates wonderful platters of charcuterie featuring Serrano ham, Dunbarton blue cheese, and wild boar. Small plates, ideal for sharing, include a grilled vegetable tart with feta and a Cabernet reduction, crispy local oysters with mango pepper relish, and salt cod croquettes with orange saffron aioli. The large-plate menu is imaginative: Rabbit orecchiette

vies for your attention as does the grilled Thai pork belly.

Desserts are extraordinary. The goat cheesecake, for example, is paired with candied rhubarb one night. When you return, that memorable cheesecake might be topped with roasted quince or Concord grapes.

All this is offered in a serene setting. Wheat-colored walls are trimmed in crisp white over cork flooring. The dining room is spacious and airy with fun art on the walls. Up one more floor, and you're in the bar and lounge area. The signature cocktail list, created by consultant Jerri Banks, makes use of fresh herbs and exotic flavorings.

The final ingredient in this recipe for the good life is the well-thought-out wine list, one that includes niche artisan wines of the highest caliber, thanks to Jeff Callaghan. He and his wife, Geremie, are the owners of Fluke, where their passion for food, wine, and hospitality is on display every night.

Tuna Tartare with Wasabi Crème

(MAKES ABOUT 2 CUPS)

1 pound fresh sushi-grade tuna, chopped fine
Dressing (recipe follows)
Wasabi crème (recipe follows)

For the dressing:

1 cup mayonnaise
1 bunch scallions, sliced thin
¼ cup soy sauce
⅛ cup mirin
⅛ cup sake
¼ cup sriracha
1 teaspoon salt

For the wasabi crème:

1 tablespoon wasabi powder
1 teaspoon water
¼ cup crème fraîche

1 tablespoon black sesame seeds
1 tablespoon white sesame seeds
Crisped wontons or rice crackers

To make the dressing: In a bowl, combine all the dressing ingredients. Mix well.

To make the wasabi crème: In a bowl, combine the wasabi powder with water to make a smooth paste. Fold the crème fraiche into the wasabi paste. Drizzle this mixture over the top of the tuna tartare.

To serve: Combine half of the dressing with the tuna. Incorporate more dressing as needed for the desired consistency. Drizzle the Wasabi Crème over the top of the tuna tartare.

Sprinkle with black and white sesame seeds. Serve with crisped wontons or rice crackers.

FLUKE WITH CHARRED YELLOW TOMATO VINAIGRETTE, RATATOUILLE & COUSCOUS

(SERVES 2)

Chef King's note: Fluke is also called a summer flounder. If not in season, you can substitute any kind of flounder, sea bass, or striped bass for the fluke.

2 fluke fillets, 6–7 ounces each

For the vinaigrette:

2 medium yellow heirloom tomatoes
1 shallot
2 garlic cloves
¾ cup Meyer lemon juice
¼ cup red wine vinegar
½ cup extra-virgin olive oil

For the ratatouille:

1 Japanese eggplant
1 zucchini
1 yellow squash
1 cup fava beans, shelled and blanched
Olive oil or butter, as needed
¼ cup red tomato sauce
¼ cup fresh basil, cut into thin strips (chiffonade)

For the couscous:

1 package couscous

To make the vinaigrette: Char the tomatoes under a broiler or on a grill. Once cooled, add all the vinaigrette ingredients except the olive oil to a blender, and puree until smooth. Slowly add the oil to the blender while running. Set aside.

To make the ratatouille: Cut all the vegetables for the ratatouille to the same medium-dice size. In a large skillet, sauté the cut vegetables in a little olive oil or butter until tender. Add the tomato sauce and basil. Set aside.

To make the couscous: Prepare the couscous according to directions on the package. After plating, store the leftover couscous in the refrigerator.

To make the fluke: In a large skillet, pan sear the fluke 2 minutes on each side, or until the desired doneness is reached.

To serve: Place a serving of the ratatouille on one side of plate, the couscous on another side of the plate, and the charred yellow tomato vinaigrette in a pool to the side. Place the cooked fish on top of the three components.

GOAT CHEESECAKE WITH ROASTED QUINCE

(SERVES 4–6)

Chef King's note: Quince is a fall fruit. If not available, you may substitute 1 scant pint of Concord grapes for the quince. In a saucepan, combine the grapes with 2 tablespoons of sugar and the juice of 1 lemon. Bring to a boil, and simmer until the mixture thickens. Allow to cool. Strain before use.

For the cheesecake:

8 ounces goat cheese
8 ounces cream cheese
¼ cup crème fraîche
1 egg
½ teaspoon vanilla
Roasted quince (recipe follows)

For the roasted quince: (Makes about 1 cup)

2 quince
Spiced simple syrup (recipe follows)

For the spiced simple syrup:

Equal amounts of sugar and water
1 whole vanilla bean
1 whole cardamom
1 teaspoon coriander
1 teaspoon cinnamon
1 teaspoon orange peel

To make the spiced simple syrup: Combine all the ingredients in a saucepan. Bring to a boil, and reduce to a simmer until all the sugar is dissolved, about 3 minutes. Remove from the heat, and let cool completely.

To make the roasted quince: Peel the quince and poach in the spiced simple syrup until tender. Roast the quince in a 350°F oven to caramelize the cut side of the quince. Cut the quince into bite-size pieces.

To prepare: Preheat oven to 225°F. In a bowl, combine the goat cheese, cream cheese, and crème fraîche until well incorporated. Add the egg and vanilla. Mix well. Place this mixture in a 9-inch lightly greased springform pan or mold, and bake at 225°F for 30–40 minutes.

To serve: Remove the cheesecake from the oven and unmold it on a serving plate. Top the cheesecake with the roasted quince. Or you can drizzle honey over the cheesecake.

THE MOORING SEAFOOD KITCHEN & BAR

1 SAYER'S WHARF
NEWPORT, RI 02840
(401) 846-2260
MOORINGRESTAURANT.COM
EXECUTIVE CHEF BOB BANKERT

Some restaurants come and go, but The Mooring Seafood Kitchen & Bar is a star that just keeps on shining bright. For more than twenty-five years, The Mooring has been the go-to restaurant for locals and tourists alike. Located on the historic waterfront in downtown Newport, The Mooring has one of the best locations, especially for boat lovers. This large multilevel restaurant offers dazzling views of million-dollar yachts in their berths, so close you can almost reach out and touch these beautiful sailing vessels.

You'll have many dining options at The Mooring. The seats at the raw bar are usually in high demand, affording guests an up-close view of oysters and cherrystones being expertly shucked. The lounge area has a distinct nautical feel with a fireplace to warm you on chilly nights. The indoor dining space with its dark woods has a masculine feel, while dining on the expansive mahogany deck in warm weather appeals to everyone. The big outdoor bar is a popular hangout in the summer for boaters spending the weekend in Newport. It's not unusual to spot a celebrity or two there.

One menu is in play at both lunch and dinner, courtesy of Executive Chef Bob Bankert. He worked his way up at the Newport Restaurant Group, the parent company that owns The Mooring and several other Rhode Island restaurants. Bankert started out as an intern under the tutelage of Chef Casey Riley, now the chief operating officer for the well-respected group. Bankert went on to be a sous chef, then chef tournant, and now executive chef. He is a graduate of the New England Culinary Institute.

Chef Bankert's menu is devoted to seafood, but there are dishes to satisfy anyone's palate including wonderful salads, trendy appetizers, tempting sandwiches, and even gluten-free options.

The seafood is exquisite, starting with raw bar offerings that are served impeccably. The native scallop chowder is an award winner. The Bag of Doughnuts is a fun serving of lobster, crab, and shrimp fritters in an old-fashioned brown paper bag. The baked oysters hit a new note with the use of feta as a topping. Patrons of all ages like the fish tacos served with avocado sour cream. The oyster po'boy is impressive—an oversized bun stuffed with fried oysters, grilled onions, and lemon-dill aioli.

Entrees include Portuguese roasted cod, Atlantic salmon, Maine lobster, and Georges Bank scallops. Two hard-to-resist dishes are the seafood pasta and the baked seafood pie. The pan-seared yellowfin tuna is a winner served with roasted fingerlings and bouillabaisse sauce.

Pan-Seared Yellowfin Tuna
with Bouillabaisse Sauce, Roasted Fingerling Potatoes, Braised Carrots & Leeks, Roasted Fennel & Black Olive Puree

(SERVES 6)

Accompaniments (recipes follow):

Bouillabaisse sauce
Roasted fingerling potatoes
Braised carrots & leeks
Roasted fennel
Black olive puree

For the bouillabaisse sauce:

2 tablespoons vegetable oil
1 fennel bulb, tops removed, sliced into
    thin strips (julienne)
1 Spanish onion, sliced into thin strips (julienne)
4 garlic cloves, minced
2 pounds plum tomatoes, chopped
Salt and pepper, to taste
½ bunch fresh thyme
4 bay leaves
1 cup white wine
2 cups lobster stock
Pinch saffron
¼ cup extra-virgin olive oil
1 slice good quality bread, crust removed,
    broken into pieces

For the roasted fingerling potatoes:

1 pound fingerling potatoes
Olive oil, as needed
Salt and pepper, to taste

For the braised carrots & leeks:

1 pound carrots, peeled and ends removed
4 tablespoons butter
1 bunch leeks, green ends removed, cut into
    thin strips (julienne)
Salt, to taste
¼ cup white wine
¼ cup water

For the roasted fennel:

1 fennel bulb, with the fennel tops (fronds) set aside
Olive oil, as needed
Salt and pepper, to taste

For the black olive puree:

1 cup kalamata olives, pitted
½ cup water

For the tuna:

2 pounds fresh yellowfin tuna, cut into
    6 (8-ounce) portions
Salt and pepper, to taste
Canola oil, as needed

To make the bouillabaisse sauce: In a heavy-duty saucepot, combine the vegetable oil, fennel, onions, and garlic. Sweat over low to medium heat, being careful to avoid any browning of the vegetables. Add the tomatoes and continue to cook for 10–15 minutes. Season with salt and pepper.

Tie the thyme and bay leaves in cheesecloth or a coffee filter, and add to the pot with the white wine, lobster stock, and saffron. Season again with salt and pepper. Bring to a simmer and cook until the liquid is reduced by about half. This should take about 20 minutes. Remove from the heat and allow to cool slightly.

Remove the bundle of herbs from the mixture. Puree the mixture in a blender until smooth, and then while blender is still on, drizzle in the olive oil and add the pieces of bread. This will help thicken and enrich the sauce.

Strain through a fine mesh strainer and reserve. Season with salt and pepper, if needed.

To make the roasted fingerling potatoes: Simmer the potatoes in a pot of salted boiling water until the potatoes are just tender. Strain and set aside to cool.

Preheat oven to 400°F.

Cut the potatoes in half lengthwise. Toss with olive oil, salt and pepper, and roast in a 400°F oven until golden brown. Set aside to reserve.

To make the braised carrots & leeks: Thinly slice the carrots on an angle, preferably on a mandoline.

In a saucepot, melt the butter and add the leeks. Season with salt. Sweat over medium heat, avoiding any browning, until leeks are tender. Add the sliced carrots, white wine, and water. Cook until the carrots are just tender, but still have a slight bite to them. Season again with salt, if needed.

To make the roasted fennel: Preheat oven to 350°F.

Thinly slice the fennel on an angle, preferably on a mandoline. Toss the fennel with enough olive oil to coat, and season with salt and pepper. Spread out the sliced fennel on a baking sheet and roast in a 350°F oven, stirring every few minutes, until the fennel is a light golden brown. Remove the baking sheet from the oven. Set the fennel aside to cool.

In a bowl, combine an equal amount of fennel fronds and roasted fennel, toss together, and then set aside.

To make the black olive puree: In a blender, puree the olives and water until smooth. Strain through a fine mesh strainer and set aside.

To make the tuna: Season the tuna with salt and pepper. Heat a skillet or cast-iron pan over high heat. Pour a small amount of canola oil into the pan, just enough to coat the bottom. Heat until the oil starts to smoke. Add the tuna to the pan and sear on all sides. For rare, sear for 30 seconds to 1 minute on each side. Remove the tuna from the pan, slice and serve.

Presentation: Assemble all the components of this dish as you desire. At The Mooring, the plating begins with coating each warm dinner plate with the bouillabaisse sauce. Place some of the fingerling potatoes on the sauce. Top the potatoes with the braised carrots and leeks. Shingle slices of the tuna across the top of the cooked vegetables, and place the roasted fennel and fronds on top of the tuna. Drizzle each plate with some of the black olive puree.

MUSE

VANDERBILT GRACE HOTEL
41 MARY STREET
NEWPORT, RI 02840
(401) 846-6200
GRACEHOTELS.COM
EXECUTIVE CHEF JONATHAN CARTWRIGHT

There are restaurants, and then there are RESTAURANTS. Muse is one of those RESTAURANTS, undoubtedly one of the very best places to dine in the entire state, thanks to Jonathan Cartwright, the group chef de cuisine for Grace Hotels. Muse is the centerpiece restaurant at the Vanderbilt Grace Hotel in Newport. Grace properties are located around the globe, including the famed White Barn Inn in Kennebunkport, Maine, a rare five-star restaurant according to AAA and Forbes.

Muse is an intimate restaurant with a dozen or so tables in a grand blue and white dining room with a handsome fireplace and majestic coffered ceilings. The tables are set with crisp white linens, sparkling glassware, and Baccarat crystal table lamps. The extraordinary food and polished service are equally impeccable.

A perfect dining experience at Muse might begin with the silky lobster bisque with crispy lobster wontons and cognac crème fraîche, or for pure extravagance the butter-poached smoked lobster with paprika butter sauce. When your server removes the domed lid from this dish, ghost-like clouds rise and emit a smoky perfume. You will be impressed.

Your dinner would continue with an intermezzo course of sorbet or chilled soup. The main course might be a rack of wild boar or pancetta-glazed beef tenderloin. Ethereal desserts await you: goat cheesecake with grilled peaches, flourless dark chocolate cake with caramelized white chocolate ice cream, or perhaps a selection of local and imported cheeses with fruit and house-made chutney.

The unusual menu also allows guests to create their own dining experience, simpler combinations of meat or seafood with basic side dishes and a choice of classic sauces. For example, you might select a duck breast with smoky fig sauce and basmati rice, or salmon with sweet spicy soy sauce and steamed broccoli.

If you are in luck, Chef Cartwright might be on the premises when you dine at Muse, but chances are his well-trained staff will be in charge of your dinner that night. The globe-trotting chef, who makes his home in Maine, might very well be tending to new Grace hotels in Argentina or Panama.

LOBSTER BISQUE

(MAKES 2 QUARTS)

For the lobster stock:

Several pounds of lobster shells (available at
    fish markets)
Olive oil, as needed
Onion, carrot, and celery, cut into large chunks
1 tablespoon peppercorns
2 bay leaves
Several parsley sprigs
Cold water, as needed

For the bisque:

4 tablespoons (½ stick) unsalted butter
1 medium onion, diced
1 garlic clove
6 medium tomatoes, diced
1 sprig fresh thyme
1 sprig fresh parsley
1 sprig fresh tarragon
½ cup white dessert wine, such as Muscat
1 cup brandy
4 cups heavy cream
4 cups lobster stock (recipe follows)
1 teaspoon lobster roe, if available
Salt, freshly ground pepper, and cayenne, to taste
Juice of ½ lemon

To make the lobster stock: Preheat oven to 400°F. Brush the lobster shells with a little olive oil. Crush the shells a bit with a meat mallet or hammer. Roast the shells in a 400°F oven for 30 minutes, or until they are bright red. Combine the roasted shells with the remaining ingredients in a large stockpot, including enough cold water to cover all the shells. Bring to a simmer. Simmer for 2 hours. Strain the mixture. You can store the lobster stock in the refrigerator for 1 week or in the freezer for 3 months.

To make the bisque: In a large saucepan with a heavy bottom, melt the butter over medium heat. Add the onion, garlic, tomatoes, and herbs, and sauté for about 5 minutes, until the onions are translucent but not browned.

Add the wine and brandy, and increase the heat to medium high, cooking the mixture until it is reduced by half. Add the cream and lobster stock, and bring to a boil. Reduce the heat to medium and cook for about 15 minutes, whisking occasionally, until it is thick enough to coat the back of a spoon.

Whisk in the lobster roe, if available, and bring the soup back to a boil. Strain the soup through a fine sieve into a clean saucepan. Season to taste with salt, pepper, cayenne, and lemon juice before serving.

Author's note: You can easily make your own lobster stock, or you can purchase it online at amazon.com. Three brands to try are Glace de Fruits de Mer Gold (excellent but expensive), Bar Harbor All Natural Maine Lobster Stock (for a fresh-off-the-docks taste), and Better than Bouillon Lobster Base (best value).

SMOKED KENNEBUNKPORT LOBSTER WITH PAPRIKA BUTTER SAUCE

(SERVES 4)

For the lobster:

¼ cup cognac

½ cup Quady Essencia wine, or your favorite
   dessert wine

½ cup lobster stock

3 cups heavy cream

8 ounces (2 sticks) cold unsalted butter, diced

2 tablespoons lobster coral (roe)

Salt and cayenne pepper, to taste

2 teaspoons paprika

½ lemon, for juice

4 parsnips, peeled and diced small

½ cup heavy cream

2 (1½ pound) lobsters, steamed with the meat
   removed from the shell

Beurre fondue, as needed

Paprika Butter Sauce (recipe follows), for garnish

Applewood chips and a smoking gun

For the paprika butter sauce:

8 ounces (2 sticks) butter, melted

1½ teaspoons salt

Paprika, to taste

To make the vegetable base: In a thick-bottomed pan, reduce the cognac, Essencia, and lobster stock by half. Add the cream and reduce by half. Whisk in the cold diced unsalted butter and reserved lobster coral. Season to taste with salt and cayenne pepper. Mix in the paprika and a few drops of lemon juice. Strain and keep warm.

Place the parsnips in a saucepan over medium-high heat. Cover with cream and bring to a simmer for 30 minutes. Strain and reserve liquid. Place the parsnips in a blender, and puree while you slowly add the reserved liquid to make a fluid puree. Season with salt and cayenne pepper. Set aside. Keep warm.

(At Muse, the vegetable base of this dish changes with the seasons. In the summer, it might be a sweet corn puree. In the fall, it would be a parsnip puree.)

To make the paprika butter sauce: In a sauté pan over low heat, combine the butter with the salt and paprika. Blend well.

To prepare the lobster: Gently poach the lobster meat in a beurre fondue until warm. (Beurre fondue is an emulsified blend of water and melted butter that is used as a poaching liquid. Combine ½ inch of simmering water with 2 sticks of melted butter and 1½ teaspoons of salt.) Place the poached lobster on top of a streak of the parsnip puree. Drizzle the paprika butter sauce around the lobster.

If possible, use a smoking gun (available at restaurant supply stores) and wood chips to create an aromatic smoke effect when this dish is served. It's best if this dish is served with a domed cover or lid to contain the smoke. Upon serving the dish, remove the dome for a very impressive presentation.

Since 1981, Newport has been the site of the Great Chowder Cook-Off, the longest-running chowder competition in the nation. Featured on the Food Network and the Travel Channel, this legendary event draws thousands of chowder lovers who, for a set fee of around $25, get to taste as much chowder as they desire from dozens of participating restaurants from across the country. (Children under age twelve get in for free with an adult.) Traditional and innovative chowders are sampled, and then attendees vote for the best in three categories: clam chowder, seafood chowder, and most creative chowder. The winning restaurants go home with prizes and bragging rights for the year.

In 2013, the only local winner was the Melville Grille in Portsmouth for its seafood chowder. Stefano's Seafood Restaurant in New Jersey won for its clam chowder, and the Octagon Restaurant in Connecticut won for its creative chowder.

In recent years, the Newport Oyster Festival has been a new facet of the chowder cook-off with local shellfish and seafood presented in a farmers' market–type setting, along with beverages and live music.

The Great Chowder Cook-Off is always held, rain or shine, on the first Saturday in June. For more information, visit newportwaterfrontevents.com.

RHODE ISLAND QUAHOG CHOWDER (IN A CLEAR BROTH)

(SERVES 20)

Rhode Islanders whose forebears were early settlers in the state would never put anything but quahogs into a chowder. (If you are unable to obtain quahogs at the seafood market, you can purchase cans of chopped clams in major supermarkets—but we can't guarantee the chowder will be quite as good.) This old Yankee recipe has been handed down from generation to generation. It makes a zesty, clear-broth chowder.

16 cups (1 gallon) clam juice (available in bottles and cans in major supermarkets)
¼ pound salt pork, chopped
½ cup diced onions
8 pounds all-purpose potatoes, peeled and diced in ½-inch pieces
1 tablespoon white pepper
1 tablespoon Worcestershire sauce
2 cups chopped, cooked quahogs

In a large stockpot, heat the clam juice just to simmer, then cover and set aside.

In a frying pan, fry the salt pork. When the fat is cooked out, remove the salt pork and set aside. Sauté the onions in the fat until they are translucent. Do not allow the onions to brown.

Put the stockpot back on the heat. Add the onions to the clam juice and bring to a simmer. Add the potatoes and simmer until tender. Add the fried salt pork, pepper, and Worcestershire sauce. Add the chopped quahogs; heat through and serve.

ONE BELLEVUE AT THE HOTEL VIKING

ONE BELLEVUE AVENUE
NEWPORT, RI 02840
(401) 848-4813
HOTELVIKING.COM
EXECUTIVE CHEF KEVIN THIELE

The Hotel Viking has a fascinating history. It was built in the 1920s by the citizens of Newport to accommodate visitors to this city-by-the-sea. The "people's hotel" has hosted many famous guests over the decades, from the Astors and Vanderbilts to President and Mrs. John F. Kennedy and modern-day celebrities. The historic hotel is located at one end of Bellevue Avenue, the address for Newport's famous mansions, which were "summer cottages" for the wealthiest Americans a century ago. Today those mansions are open to the public desiring a glimpse of Newport's gilded age.

Within Hotel Viking is One Bellevue, a fine-dining restaurant that combines classic elegance with the modern cuisine of Executive Chef Kevin Thiele. Known especially for its seafood, One Bellevue also has an award-winning wine list. The restaurant is famous for its Afternoon Tea complete with tea sandwiches, tea breads, and house-made scones served with lemon cream and preserves.

As a hotel, One Bellevue is open daily for breakfast, lunch, and dinner. Breakfast might consist of a Newport omelet filled with lobster, artichokes, and chèvre cheese. A satisfying lunch could consist of lump crab cakes with jalapeño aioli along with the chef's Grand Chowder teeming with clams, lobster, scallops, and shrimp. For dinner, one could begin with the wasabi steak tartare, followed with the cider-glazed roasted chicken served with pancetta whipped potatoes. All this is served by an impeccably trained staff, which is what you'd expect at a hotel restaurant of this stature.

Dining areas include the Salon and the Garden Room, quietly elegant in varying shades of cream and gold. In warm weather, the Garden Patio is the place to be, especially when the sun goes down and the outdoor fireplace is lit—the perfect spot after a day of sightseeing in trendy Newport.

A New Jersey native, Thiele graduated with a bachelor's degree in culinary arts from Johnson & Wales University. His early career led him to jobs in Ireland, Germany, and Martha's Vineyard. He started as a line cook at One Bellevue in 2004, and he was elevated to chef in less than three years. The award-winning chef loves the cuisines of Asia, France, and Italy, but he is dedicated to New England regional specialties and locally sourced, seasonal food.

An interesting tidbit: The name of the Hotel Viking derives from the legendary lore of the Nordic Vikings who are believed to have landed in Newport around AD 1000, long before Christopher Columbus discovered America.

WASABI STEAK TARTARE
WITH PICKLED CUCUMBER SALAD & SOY GLAZE

(SERVES 2)

1 cucumber

2 tablespoons rice wine vinegar

1 teaspoon granulated sugar

3 teaspoons sea salt, divided

½ pound prime grade filet mignon, diced small
    (⅛-inch cubes)

1 tablespoon minced scallions

1 teaspoon prepared wasabi (equal parts wasabi
    powder and water)

1 teaspoon extra virgin olive oil

½ ounce pea sprouts, for garnish

1 tablespoon soy glaze (see chef's note)

1 (2 x 2-inch) wonton sheet, cut into strips and
    baked (optional)

Cut the cucumber in half. Dice one half of the cucumber into small ⅛-inch cubes, and set aside in a bowl. Using a mandoline, slice the other half of the cucumber lengthwise into very thin strips. Place these strips in a separate bowl. Add the vinegar, sugar, and 1 teaspoon of sea salt to the strips. Mix together and set aside to marinate.

Place the diced filet mignon in the bowl of diced cucumbers. Add the scallions, prepared wasabi, olive oil, and remaining sea salt. Mix together lightly until all the ingredients are evenly incorporated.

Chef Thiele's note: To make the soy glaze, combine ¼ cup of soy sauce and ¼ cup of brown sugar in a saucepan over medium heat. Stir to dissolve the sugar. Continue to cook until the mixture is reduced by half. Store any unused soy glaze in the refrigerator for future use.

Place a 3-inch ring mold in the center of each dinner plate. Lightly pack the tartare into the ring mold. Carefully lift and remove the ring mold. Top the tartare with the pickled cucumbers and pea sprouts. Drizzle the soy glaze on and around the tartare. Garnish with the baked wonton strips (if desired).

Cider-Glazed Chicken with Pancetta Whipped Potatoes & Morel Mushrooms

(SERVES 2)

For the cider glaze:

1 quart apple cider
1 cup brown sugar
1 cinnamon stick
1 star anise

For the pancetta potatoes:

2 Idaho potatoes, peeled and diced
2 tablespoons heavy cream
1 tablespoon unsalted butter
Salt and pepper, to taste
¼ cup diced pancetta
1 teaspoon parsley

For the chicken:

2 chicken breasts, with skin left on
Salt and pepper, to taste
Olive oil, as needed

For the morels:

1 tablespoon olive oil
6 morel caps
Salt and pepper, to taste
1 teaspoon thyme

To make the cider glaze: Preheat oven to 375°F.

Combine all the ingredients for the cider glaze in a saucepan over medium heat. Stirring every 15 minutes, reduce until slightly thickened. Strain the cider reduction through a fine sieve, and set the cider glaze aside until needed.

To make the pancetta potatoes: Cook the diced potatoes in boiling water until tender. Drain the potatoes. Place the cooked potatoes in a bowl with the cream, butter, salt and pepper. Mash the potatoes.

In a large frying pan, render the pancetta over low to medium heat until all the fat has melted and the pancetta is crispy. Add the mashed potatoes and parsley to the pan. Mix well. Cover the pan to keep the pancetta potatoes hot.

To make the chicken: Season the chicken on both sides with salt and pepper. In a cast-iron skillet or regular frying pan on high heat, sear the chicken skin-side down in a little olive oil. When golden brown, flip the chicken over and finish cooking in the preheated oven for 20 minutes.

To make the morels: In a sauté pan, heat the 1 tablespoon of olive oil. When the pan is hot, add the morels. Season with salt and pepper. Remove from the heat and add the thyme. Set aside.

When the chicken is done, remove from the oven. Allow the chicken to rest on a cutting board.

To serve: Place a heaping scoop of the pancetta potatoes in the center of each dinner plate. Cut the chicken into 1-inch pieces on a bias, and place the chicken strips on top of the potatoes. Place the morels to the side of the chicken. Glaze the chicken with the cider reduction. Drizzle the reminder of the glaze around the plate for a beautiful presentation.

Tallulah on Thames

464 Thames Street
Newport, RI 02840
(401) 849-2433
TALLULAHONTHAMES.COM
Executive Chef Jake Rojas

Jake Rojas is fascinating. He is the executive chef and an owner of Tallulah on Thames, where his delicate plates of food are almost too beautiful to eat. He also creates some of the best Mexican street food in the state. It's a curious juxtaposition of cuisines, and one that everyone should experience.

His artful food is served at night at Tallulah's, a historic storefront corner restaurant. Modern, fresh, local—that is the chef's mantra. Rojas is committed to sourcing seasonal ingredients from local farms and artisans so that he and his talented team can create delightful dining experiences. You can watch that team in action through a wide window into the kitchen. Above the window are a slew of cookbooks, most of them obviously well used over the years. At night, this restaurant is elegant with a Parisian black-and-white color scheme and super-plush dining room chairs. Even the staff is clad in black-and-white-striped aprons and print bandanas.

A typical dinner menu might offer a corn velouté, heirloom tomatoes, and duck confit as appetizers, with each dish precisely prepared. When Chef Rojas makes his lamb-stuffed piquillo peppers, he likes to use the underutilized neck of the lamb. For an entree, vegetarians will like the carrot agnolotti with its hint of ginger. The simple roasted chicken

would appeal to me. Other options are scallops, striped bass, swordfish, and hanger steak, with each one having unique accompaniments. The pan-roasted native monkfish is another work of art. A sweet or savory ending to dinner would be lemon cheesecake with honey-ginger crumble or a heavenly cheese plate with seasonal jam.

From fall into spring, every Wednesday is Burger Night at Tallulah's, very affordable with the Black Angus beef coming from Blackbird Farm in Smithfield. Similarly, Sunday Suppers are offered with a three-course prix-fixe dinner available at a low price. But these specials are suspended when the busy tourist season returns to Newport for the summer.

By day, Tallulah on Thames has a stripped-down look in the dining room with the kitchen creating the most incredible tacos I've ever had. The food is served on paper plates to tables covered with green plastic tablecloths. At first, it's almost shocking—a complete change in personality. But this is the food Chef Rojas grew up on in his hometown of El Paso, Texas. His burritos and *tortas* can also be had in gluten-free and vegetarian preparations. In the warm summer months, Chef Rojas also mans a taco stand in nearby Jamestown, and he has plans to open Tallulah's Taqueria, a taco restaurant in Providence.

Chef Rojas has an impressive résumé. Prior to his move to Rhode Island (where his wife is from), Rojas was a chef at restaurants in Malibu, Las Vegas, Boca Raton, and West Palm Beach, working under influential celebrity chefs. They obviously ignited a passion for food in Jake Rojas.

PIQUILLO PEPPERS STUFFED
WITH HOPKINS FARM LAMB

(MAKES 24 STUFFED PEPPERS)

3-pound deboned leg of lamb
Sea salt and white pepper, to taste
2 cups diced carrots
2 cups diced onions
¼ cup tomato paste
1 cup sherry vinegar
4 cups red wine
2 quarts chicken stock
30 piquillo peppers

Author's note: The piquillo pepper from Spain is
a variety of chile with a sweet taste and no heat.
They are roasted over hot embers, peeled, and
deseeded by hand, and then packed into tins
or jars for sale. Often served as tapas, they are
usually stuffed with meat, seafood, or cheese.
Tallulah on Thames obtains its lamb from Hopkins
Farm in North Scituate, Rhode Island.

Preheat oven to 300°F.

Place a large roasting pan or pot over medium
heat. Season the leg of lamb with sea salt and
white pepper. Place the lamb in the roasting pan,
and sear until caramelized on all sides. Remove
the lamb and add the carrots and onions. Cook
until caramelized. Reduce the heat to low and
add the tomato paste. Mix well. Cook until
aromatic.

Add the sherry vinegar, and increase the heat to
medium. Cook until the sauce has thickened.

Add the red wine and chicken stock, and bring
to a boil. Return the lamb to the roasting pan.
Cover with foil and braise in the 300°F oven for
2–3 hours, or until the meat is easily shredded.
Remove the meat from the pan, and set aside.

Strain the braising liquid into a medium-size
pot, and reduce the liquid by half over low heat.
Season to taste with salt and pepper. Keep
warm.

Allow the lamb to cool down, and shred the meat.
Season with salt and pepper. Stuff the shredded
lamb into the peppers. Drizzle a little bit of the
reduced braising liquid over the peppers just
before serving.

Pan-Roasted Native Monkfish, Lentils du Puy, Fennel & Blood Orange Salad

(SERVES 4)

Chef Rojas's note: Monkfish needs to be cleaned, if bought with its skin on or off. Remove the skin by wrapping a kitchen towel around the front of the filet and peel it back. Once the skin is off, use a sharp knife to trim off all the under-skin membrane and the bloodline. If buying already cleaned fillets, season with sea salt and white pepper before cooking. We like to sprinkle fennel pollen over the fillets when done cooking. This adds an extraordinary depth of flavor.

For the monkfish:

1 tablespoon oil
4 (8-ounce) monkfish fillets
4 tablespoons unsalted butter
1 lemon, cut into quarters

For the lentils: (Makes 8 servings)

1 cup diced bacon
2 cups finely diced onions
1 cup finely diced fennel
2 cups lentils
1 cup white wine
8 cups chicken stock
2 cups finely diced carrots
2 tablespoons unsalted butter
Salt and white pepper, to taste
1 tablespoon chopped parsley
1 tablespoon chopped chives
¼ cup sherry vinegar, preferably vinagre de Jerez

For the fennel & blood orange salad:

1 fennel bulb with tops still on (remove tops and save
    for garnish)
2 chioggia beets or golden beets
3 blood oranges
⅓ cup blood orange juice
⅔ cup olive oil
1 tablespoon Dijon mustard
1 tablespoon minced shallots

To make the lentils: In a medium to large saucepot over medium to high heat, cook the bacon until caramelized, constantly stirring.

Add the diced onions and fennel. Stir in the lentils. Deglaze the pot with white wine and reduce by half. Add the chicken stock and bring to a boil.

Turn the heat down to low and simmer for 15 minutes. Add the carrots and continue to simmer for 5 more minutes.

When the lentils are fully cooked but still have a little bite to them, add the butter, salt, white pepper, and chopped herbs.

To finish, add the vinegar right before serving, which will brighten up the dish.

This recipe will provide more than the 4 servings needed. Refrigerate the leftover for use in another dish.

To make the fennel & blood orange salad: On a mandoline or with a vegetable peeler, shave the fennel and beets. Set aside for the salad.

Peel two oranges and slice into rounds. Break the rounds into individual segments. Reserve the segments. Over a bowl, squeeze the juice of the third orange, and use the juice to create a quick vinaigrette (see note below) in which to toss the

salad. The fennel tops can be used by picking some of the fronds to use as a garnish.

Chef Rojas's note: To make a quick vinaigrette, combine one part blood orange juice with two parts olive oil in a blender or food processor. Add a little Dijon mustard and some minced shallots. Blend until incorporated. Season to taste with salt and pepper.

To make the monkfish: Preheat oven to 350°F.

In a large sauté pan over high heat, add the oil. Lay the seasoned fillets in the pan, presentation side down. Sear until golden brown and caramelized. Flip the fillets over and continue to sear. Turn the heat down to medium-low, and add the unsalted butter and baste for 1 minute. Remove the fish from the pan and place in an ovenproof dish. Squeeze a few drops of lemon juice over the top of each fillet.

Place the fillets into the 350°F oven and continue to cook until done, approximately 3 minutes. Remove the fillets from the oven and let rest for 2 minutes. Slice the fillets just before serving. Place about 1 cup of the lentils in the center of each dinner plate. Top with a monkfish fillet. Serve the salad on a separate plate on the side.

22 Bowen's Wine Bar & Grille

Bowen's Wharf
Newport, RI 02840
(401) 841-8884
22bowens.com
Executive Chef Guy Ferri

The perfect day in Newport begins with an after-breakfast stroll along the quiet waterfront, up and down the commercial wharves. Since it is early in the day, tourists are in short supply. Shopkeepers are starting their morning ritual of opening up for business. Beautifully restored schooners glide out into Newport Harbor for their first tour of the day. Around 11 a.m., the restaurants begin to stir, at least those that are open for lunch. It's much like backstage at the theater with people scurrying about, getting everything in place before the curtain rises. It's show time!

One of the best shows around is at 22 Bowen's Wine Bar & Grille, part of the prestigious Newport Restaurant Group. This is a big restaurant with dining on two levels and an outdoor patio called Portside that sits on the dock right next to the tall sailing ships. 22 Bowen's—as it is called by regular customers—has a formally set interior with

dark woods and a brick floor. Nautical prints adorn the walls. A world-class steakhouse, 22 Bowen's is also known for its seafood and an award-winning wine list.

Executive Chef Guy Ferri is in charge of the semi-open kitchen. A native of New Jersey, Chef Ferri found his way to Newport after career stops in San Francisco and New York. His food is artfully presented, from a colorful chicken cobb salad for lunch to the yellowfin tuna at dinner. One of the most popular menu items is the Bucket of Clams, a stainless steel bucket containing a variety of native clams and mussels in their natural broth with drawn butter on the side and grilled bread for sopping up every last drop.

But meat is the star of this show, especially the USDA prime steaks aged to perfection. All steaks and chops are served with a choice of toothsome sauces: béarnaise, roasted garlic beurre blanc, bordelaise, and blue cheese butter, to name just some. Even the burgers are special, especially the eight-ounce prime burger served on a house-made brioche bun with foie gras aioli. Side dishes are just as indulgent, including the wild mushroom fricassee, creamed spinach, and perhaps the best mac and cheese on earth.

Bucket of Clams

(SERVES 2)

¼ cup extra-virgin olive oil

1 teaspoon minced garlic

8 littleneck clams, washed

½ cup white wine

Juice from 1 lemon

8 soft-shell steamer clams, washed

8 local mussels, washed

1 tablespoon butter

Salt and pepper, to taste

1 tablespoon chopped parsley

1 baguette

Olive oil, as needed

In a small pot, heat the olive oil and lightly sauté the garlic for about 30 seconds to release the aroma. Add the littleneck clams first, as they take the longest to open. Add the wine and lemon juice and begin to steam the clams. After 3 minutes, add the steamer clams and steam for 2 minutes. Add the mussels, butter, salt, and pepper. Steam for 2 minutes, or until all the shellfish opens. Sprinkle with the chopped parsley.

Slice the baguette into 1-inch-thick slices and brush each slice with olive oil. Lightly grill or toast the bread in an oven and serve with the steamed shellfish.

Serve the shellfish in a stainless steel pail or a large bowl for sharing, or divide the shellfish and broth evenly between two bowls. Serve with the grilled bread.

WHITE HORSE TAVERN

26 MARLBOROUGH STREET
NEWPORT, RI 02840
(401) 849-3600
WHITEHORSENEWPORT.COM
EXECUTIVE CHEF RICH SILVIA

Dinner at the White Horse Tavern is on the bucket list of many a foodie, especially those with a love of history. The White Horse Tavern is the quintessential colonial Newport building with its dark red clapboard exterior, gambrel roof, plain pediment doors, huge interior wood beams, narrow staircase, and cavernous fireplaces. Built as a two-story private residence in 1652, the structure was converted to a tavern in 1673.

Back in the seventeenth century, few people could read, and they relied on symbols instead of words. The symbol for a tavern was a white horse painted on a wooden sign. That's how the White Horse Tavern got its name. It was a regular meeting place for colonists, British soldiers, pirates, and sailors. In 1708, city officials began to dine there, and thus the businessman's lunch was born. If only those dark green walls could talk—you can't help but wonder as you make your way through the various dining rooms into the intimate pub room, with the wide-plank floorboards beneath you creaking with every step. Antique prints and lantern sconces hang on the wall. It makes for an unforgettable dining experience.

Executive Chef Rich Silvia respects the historic setting of the White Horse Tavern, and his menu offers delicious old classics with a dash of contemporary cuisine. On the tried-and-true side, you'll find New England clam chowder, salt cod fritters, foie gras, and escargots. For this new millennium, you can dine on sushi-grade tuna tartare tacos, lobster mac and cheese, and roasted vegetable ravioli.

One of the most popular items on the menu is the beef Wellington encased in puff pastry over potato puree alongside baby vegetables. If you're lucky, the chef's famous Scotch eggs will be on the menu when you dine at the White Horse. He offers this traditional British picnic food as an appetizer, a memorable one indeed made with duck eggs.

Chef Silvia embraces the local food scene, pairing the best artisan cheeses with Aquidneck Island honeycomb, and buying fresh seafood right off the boats that land in Newport Harbor. A native Rhode Islander, Chef Silvia started his career in 2001 as the executive sous chef at the White Horse Tavern. He also worked as the chef at the prestigious Vanderbilt Hall Hotel and Carnegie Abbey Club and at Johnson & Wales University before rejoining the White Horse as its executive chef in 2009.

Scotch Eggs
with Honey Bourbon Sauce & Sriracha

(SERVES 6)

For the Scotch eggs:

1 tablespoon salt

1 tablespoon white vinegar

6 duck eggs

6 (2-ounce) prepared duck sausages (available at
upscale butcher shops and online at dartagnan.com)

1 cup all-purpose flour

2 duck eggs, whipped with 2 tablespoons water

2 cups panko bread crumbs, crushed fine

2 quarts canola oil, for frying

Kosher salt and freshly ground black pepper, to taste

For the honey bourbon sauce:

1 cup homemade or good quality commercial
mayonnaise

½ cup honey bourbon or honey whiskey

1 tablespoon honey

1 tablespoon lemon juice

Kosher salt and white pepper, to taste

For the garnish:

Sriracha chile sauce, as needed

4 ounces pea tendrils

Salt and pepper, to taste

To make the Scotch eggs: Fill a medium
saucepan with water, salt, and white vinegar.
When the water is boiling, use a spoon to gently
lower the 6 duck eggs in the pan. Set a timer and
cook for 8 minutes.

Remove the eggs from the pan. Rinse the
eggs under cold water until the eggs are cool
enough to handle with your hands (do not cool
completely at this point as the shells will stick to
the egg). Peel the eggs and immediately place
them in a bowl of ice water to chill completely.
Once chilled, remove the eggs from the water
and dry completely.

Remove the duck sausage from the casings, and flatten out into even circles, 1 sausage for each egg. Place a boiled duck egg in the center of each sausage disk and wrap the sausage meat around the egg completely. Once all are complete, place them back in the refrigerator to chill until the sausage is firm again.

Set up a standard breading station by placing the flour, beaten egg mixture, and panko into three separate bowls. Remove the boiled eggs from the refrigerator. Dredge them first in the flour using one hand, and then using your other hand toss them completely in the beaten egg mixture. Remove the eggs from the egg mixture, and coat them thoroughly with the panko bread crumbs. Refrigerate again until they become firm.

Heat the canola oil to 350°F. Drop in the coated eggs one or two at a time, and fry until golden brown and the sausage is cooked, about 4–6 minutes. Remove the eggs from the oil, and allow them to rest on paper towels. Season with salt and pepper.

To make the honey-bourbon sauce: Combine all of the ingredients, and season to taste with salt and pepper.

Spoon an equal amount of the honey-bourbon sauce in the center of a decorative bowl or small plate. Swipe a small decorative line of sriracha on the rim of the plate. Add a good pinch of the pea tendrils seasoned with salt and pepper to the center top of the circle of sauce. Slice each Scotch egg in half lengthwise and present in the center of the sauce with the yolks facing up.

Beef Wellington with Sauce Périgueux

(SERVES 6)

For the Périgueux sauce:

1 tablespoons canola oil
1 tablespoon minced shallot
¼ cup Madeira wine
1⅓ cups veal demi-glacé (available in upscale
    butcher shops)
1 tablespoon black truffle juice
1 tablespoon minced black truffle, canned or fresh
Kosher salt and freshly ground black pepper, to taste

For the beef Wellingtons:

6 (5-ounce) prime or choice filet mignon steaks
Kosher salt and freshly ground black pepper, to taste
2 tablespoons canola oil
1½ sheets puff pastry
9 ounces truffled foie gras pâté
2 large egg yolks beaten with 2 tablespoons water

For the side vegetables:

6 baby carrots, precooked
12 haricots verts (French green beans), precooked
12 asparagus stalks, precooked
Butter, as needed
Salt and pepper, to taste
Mashed potatoes, enough for 6 servings

To make the sauce Périgueux: In a small, heavy saucepan, heat the oil over medium heat, and sauté the shallots until translucent, about 3 minutes. Add the Madeira wine, and cook until it is reduced to a syrup-like consistency. Add the demi-glacé and truffle juice, and simmer until it coats a spoon lightly. Add the minced truffles. Season with salt and pepper to taste. Remove from the heat, cover, and keep warm.

To make the beef Wellingtons: Season the filets liberally on both sides with salt and pepper. In a large sauté pan, heat the oil over a medium-high heat and sear the filets on each side for 1 minute for rare. Transfer the meat to a wire rack to cool. Refrigerate for at least an hour.

Cut the one whole sheet of puff pastry into 6 equal squares, and spread them out on a work surface. Add an equal amount of the paté to the center of each square, then top each with a cooled filet. Pull all four corners of the pastry together at the top and seal them well. Brush the entire outside of the puff pastry with the egg yolk mixture to coat evenly.

Place the half sheet of puff pastry on the counter and cut out decorative shapes to top each Beef Wellington.

Preheat the oven to 450°F.

Spray a baking sheet with cooking spray, and arrange the beef Wellingtons on the prepared pan. Bake on the center rack of the oven for 20 minutes for medium rare steaks. Remove from the oven and allow to rest for 3–4 minutes.

To make the vegetables: While the beef Wellingtons are baking, heat the vegetables in a small amount of melted butter, and season with salt and pepper. The mashed potatoes are prepared in advance and are kept warm on the stove over low heat.

To plate: Put an equal amount of the sauce in the center of each plate. Spoon a small amount of mashed potatoes in the center on top of the sauce. Arrange the vegetables leaning against the potatoes, and place the Beef Wellington against the potatoes and vegetables.

SOUTH COUNTY

Coast Guard House

40 Ocean Road
Narragansett, RI 02882
(401) 789-0700
THECOASTGUARDHOUSE.COM
Executive Chefs Angel Cardona and Ray Montaquila

First-time visitors to Narragansett are often surprised when they come upon the magical Narragansett Towers that span scenic Route 1, romantic remnants from yesteryear. Right next door is the historic Coast Guard House. Built on the rocky edge of the ocean, this restaurant was once a life-saving station for what is now the US Coast Guard. In 1945, it became a waterfront restaurant, one that has been battered and bruised by severe coastal storms, but the Coast Guard House has always survived.

Most recently, the Coast Guard House was virtually destroyed by Superstorm Sandy in late 2012. It took more than a year to rebuild this landmark restaurant. Throughout the reconstruction process, the rooftop deck remained open in fair weather, serving stellar new American cuisine.

Like other smart restaurants, the Coast Guard House has two chefs in charge of the kitchen, ensuring consistent food quality every day of the week, at lunch, at dinner, and at their famed Sunday brunch. Angel Cardona and Ray Montaquila are both responsible for a menu that offers fresh local seafood and creative dishes, such as Point Judith calamari and crab cakes with spicy aioli and cilantro chile relish.

The highlight of any visit to Narragansett in the summer is an afternoon on the deck at the Coast Guard House, offering an unbeatable panoramic view of Narragansett Town Beach and the Atlantic Ocean with Newport in the distance. Casually attired guests sip on their margaritas and frosty craft beers as they watch local surfers seek that perfect wave.

One of the most popular appetizers is the Sweet, Sour & Spicy Shrimp served in an oversized martini glass. Many guests eventually move downstairs to the completely redesigned dining room with its expansive ocean views to dine on delicacies such as grilled Block Island swordfish caught in the waters just off nearby Block Island. Not to be missed are the restaurant's legendary desserts, especially the flourless chocolate cake with port wine–soaked cherries and bittersweet chocolate mousse.

Every facet of a Coast Guard House dining experience is made perfect by a friendly, well-trained staff—reminiscent of the fine service offered on high-end cruise ships.

Sweet, Sour & Spicy Shrimp

(SERVES 8)

2 pounds white shrimp
1 green pepper, ribs removed and cut into
    fine julienne strips
1 medium red onion, peeled and cut into
    fine julienne strips
2 quarts water
1 tablespoon salt
1 cup fresh orange juice
½ cup fresh lemon juice
½ cup fresh lime juice
¾ cup ketchup
⅛ cup sriracha hot sauce
1 bunch fresh cilantro, chopped

Peel and devein the shrimp. Set the shrimp shells aside—do not discard. (The shrimp can be prepared one day in advance.) Refrigerate until needed.

Place the julienne strips of peppers and onions in a bowl of cold water.

Bring the 2 quarts of water to a boil. Add the salt and reserved shrimp shells. Reduce heat to medium low or until the water comes to a simmer. Use a strainer to lower the raw shrimp into the poaching liquid. Remove the shrimp when they are almost cooked through—do not overcook. To cool the shrimp, place them in a

bowl placed over a larger bowl of icy water. Strain the poaching liquid and set it aside.

Remove the peppers and onions from the cold water, and place them in a large bowl. Add the poached shrimp, remaining ingredients, and 2 cups of the strained poaching liquid. Mix well. If needed, season to taste with salt.

GRILLED BLOCK ISLAND SWORDFISH
WITH SCAPECE

(SERVES 4)

For the Israeli couscous:

1 cup diced red onions

¾ cup loosely packed mint

2 tablespoons red pepper flakes

¾ cup extra-virgin olive oil

3 cups Israeli couscous or *fregola*

1 quart vegetable stock

For the scapece:

½ pound swordfish pieces

2 quarts water

2 lemons, juiced

2 tablespoons salt

¾ cup extra-virgin olive oil, divided

1 cup sliced red onions, in julienne strips

3 cups diced tomatoes

1 cup diced cucumber

¼ cup red wine vinegar

⅛ cup fresh marjoram

1 tablespoon red pepper flakes

For the basil emulsion: (Makes 2 cups)

1 cup fresh basil

½ cup fresh mint

¼ cup honey

1 tablespoon red pepper flakes

3 ounces pasteurized egg yolks

¼ cup aged sherry vinegar

1 cup extra-virgin olive oil

½ cup canola oil

Salt, to taste

For the swordfish:

4 (8-ounce) swordfish steaks

Olive oil, as needed

Salt and pepper, to taste

Fresh greens (arugula or watercress), optional

To make the Israeli couscous: In a sauté pan with a wide bottom, sweat the onions, mint, and red pepper flakes in the olive oil. Lower the heat to medium, and add the couscous. Stir frequently until well toasted. Add the vegetable stock a ladle at a time and cook until the liquid is absorbed, as one would do for risotto.

When all the liquid is absorbed, the couscous is done. This should take about 10 minutes. The cooked texture should be firm, as al dente pasta would be.

To make the scapece: Cut the swordfish pieces into ¾-inch chunks, using only the firm layer of flesh located just below the skin.

In a medium saucepan, bring the water to a boil with the lemon juice, salt, and 4 tablespoons of the olive oil. Reduce the heat until the liquid comes to a simmer. Add the swordfish pieces and cook until the heat has penetrated all but the very center of each chunk. Allow the fish to cool slightly in the poaching liquid.

In a mixing bowl, combine the remaining ingredients and set aside.

While the swordfish chunks are still warm, remove them from the poaching liquid, and combine with the rest of the ingredients in the mixing bowl. Mix carefully to ensure the chunks of swordfish remain whole.

To make the basil emulsion: In a blender, combine the basil, mint, honey, red pepper flakes, egg yolks, and vinegar. On medium-high speed, puree the mixture. With the blender still running, slowly drizzle in both oils until a smooth consistency is reached. Season to taste with salt. This emulsion is similar to aioli, and it is excellent when used as a spread in sandwiches.

Chef's note: Pasteurized egg yolks are used in place of raw eggs for food safety reasons. This emulsion can be made without the pasteurized egg yolks, if desired.

To make the swordfish: Brush the swordfish steaks with oil, and season with salt and pepper. Place the steaks on the grill, and cook until done but not dry.

To plate: Spoon a generous serving of couscous onto each dinner plate, and place the grilled swordfish steak on top. Spoon the *scapece* on top of the swordfish. Drizzle the basil emulsion around the food on the plate. Finish the dish with fresh greens, if desired.

CRAZY BURGER

144 BOON STREET
NARRAGANSETT, RI 02882
(401) 783-1810
CRAZYBURGER.COM
EXECUTIVE CHEF ALEX MCBURNEY

Crazy Burger is a one-of-a-kind restaurant, unlike anything else in Rhode Island. It really is crazy in a wacky, wonderful way. Since 1995, this humble cottage in the heart of the Narragansett Pier area has been serving breakfast, lunch, and dinner. It wasn't long before customers became regulars, and fans became fanatics. During the summer, when tourists flock to this seaside town, there is almost always a line of people outside waiting for a table at Crazy Burger—even in the rain.

According to owner Mike Maxon, it's all about the food and the customer's experience. He works closely with his executive chef, Alex McBurney, on making sure the food is interesting and the dining experience unique. The young staff is quirky and friendly.

Of course, Crazy Burger is known for its burgers, but there's so much more—arguably the best breakfast in town, vegan dishes, gluten-free food, desserts made from scratch, and amazing concoctions from the juice bar. As for the twenty or so burgers on the menu, it might be easier to say what's not available.

Just some of the standout dishes include multigrain pancakes stuffed with peach compote and sweetened cream cheese for breakfast, the zucchini pancakes with chive sour cream on a bed of baby greens for lunch, and the blackened mahimahi served over spinach-corn rice with citrus-rum sauce and mango-mint salsa for dinner. Signature dishes not to be missed are the corn and sweet potato chowder, the Pacific Rim rolls with spicy Thai peanut sauce, and the baked brie filled with sun-dried tomato and artichoke pesto, baked in phyllo. Specials, such as spicy salmon cakes and apple sage sausage burgers, are posted online. This is not just a BYOB restaurant; it's a BYOBBAM restaurant—that's bring your own booze by all means—very popular on Saturday night and at Sunday brunch.

The decor is a bit bizarre with lots of mismatched cotton napkins and dishware. Colorful Chinese lanterns might be hanging from the ceiling in the main dining room—you just never know at Crazy Burger. In fair weather, a protected outdoor patio is a fun spot to dine with its jungle-like plants and vibrant wall mural.

BEAN STREET BURGER
WITH RED PEPPER CHIMICHURRI

(SERVES 8)

For the red pepper chimichurri: (Makes about 2 cups)

3 red bell peppers, chopped roughly
8 garlic cloves, peeled and left whole
¼ cup olive oil
¼ cup honey
1 bunch parsley
1 bunch cilantro
Water or olive oil, as needed

For the burgers:

4 red bell peppers, finely diced
3 cups finely diced red onions
Canola oil, as needed
2 cups black beans
½ bag frozen corn
2 cups quinoa
4 cups water
Salt, to taste
4 packages tempeh
2 cups ketchup
2 cups chimichurri
2 cups bread crumbs
Salt and pepper, to taste

To make the red pepper chimichurri: In a frying pan, sauté the red peppers and garlic in the olive oil. Add the honey, and cook over medium heat until the peppers are tender. Allow to cool.

Move the mixture into a blender. Blend until smooth, adding the parsley and cilantro in batches. If too thick, add water or more olive oil.

To make the burgers: Preheat oven to 350°F.

In a large pan, sauté the red peppers and onions in a little canola oil until soft and translucent. Stir in the black beans and corn, and simmer until heated through.

Simmer the quinoa in the water for 20 minutes. Season with salt.

In an ovenproof casserole, bake the tempeh for 20 minutes at 350°F. Allow the tempeh to cool, and crumble. Add the crumbled tempeh to the large pan, and heat through. Transfer this mixture to a large bowl.

Stir in the cooked quinoa, ketchup, chimichurri, and bread crumbs. Season with salt and pepper. Add water if mixture is too dry. Make 8 "burgers" of equal size. Since everything is already cooked, all you have to do is heat up the burgers as needed. This can be done in a frying pan with a little canola oil. When heated through, place the burgers on large buns; tortilla wraps are another excellent way to serve them.

Chef McBurney's note: At Crazy Burger, we offer about 20 different burgers, some of them vegan. All our sides, such as our sweet potato fries, are vegan as well.

CRAZY CAJUN FILET MIGNON
(SERVES 4)

1 stick unsalted butter, at room temperature
½ cup prepared horseradish
½ bunch chives, chopped
2 garlic cloves, minced
2 lemon wedges
2 teaspoons Cajun seasoning, homemade
   or store-bought
4 filet mignon steaks, of equal size
Butter, as needed for frying

Using an electric stand mixer, whip the butter with the horseradish, chives, and garlic. Squeeze the juice from the lemon wedges into the butter mixture. Mix well. With a pastry bag, pipe the butter mixture into rosettes, and refrigerate.

Rub the Cajun seasoning onto the steaks.

Preheat oven to 450°F.

In a hot cast-iron skillet, sear the steaks on both sides in a little butter until a crust forms on the meat. Move the skillet into the preheated oven. Generally speaking, every few minutes in the oven will move the steaks up a notch on the doneness scale from rare to medium to well. Depending on their size, they should never take more than another 7–8 minutes in the oven.

Remove the steaks from the oven and allow the meat to rest for 5 minutes. Top each filet mignon with a butter rosette. Serve immediately.

Chef McBurney's note: Dinner entrees at Crazy Burger are served with soup or salad. We like to serve our filet mignon with garlic mashed potatoes and grilled asparagus.

Daddy's Bread

Jennifer Hopkins Manzo
No phone, no website

A true cottage industry, Daddy's Bread at 805 Moonstone Road in Matunuck is a down-home bakery that operates on the honor system. Since 1975, this small ranch house has been stocked routinely with all kinds of baked goods made fresh daily. There is no one on the premises so customers are on their own to select their loaves of bread and fresh muffins. Prices are posted on a wall, and people tuck their dollar bills into a clearly marked payment slot that goes who knows where? People have been known to pay with winning lottery tickets. I once had to leave an IOU, only to return the next weekend with payment in hand. Many customers leave notes for Daddy.

Everett J. Hopkins was Daddy. He passed away in 2012 at the age of 83. His daughter, Jennifer Hopkins Manzo, still runs the bakery.

Outside, the house is overgrown with beach roses and vines—watch out for the poison ivy! Inside, the walls are lined with simple shelves on which more than a dozen varieties of bread sit, especially in the summer when Daddy's Bread is especially busy. White, whole wheat, 14 grain, peasant, onion chive, dark rye, apple cinnamon, apricot raisin, and the especially popular Parmesan-dill-garlic are just some of the breads. Oversized breakfast muffins are also available, but they go fast so plan on getting there early.

In the fall, Daddy's Bread is open only on weekends, and it shuts down for the winter months. Fans can't wait for this unusual bakery to reopen in the spring. There is no phone on the premises, nor is there a website. But Daddy's Bread does have a Facebook page filled with up-to-date news on what's happening at this quirky Rhode Island bakery.

Black Pearl Clam Chowder

blackpearlnewport.com

Cans of Black Pearl clam chowder—chock full of clams and creamy yellow with butter—is available online through The Black Pearl website. The Black Pearl is one of Newport's legendary waterfront restaurants with Executive Chef Daniel Knerr in charge of a kitchen that serves three dining venues: Commodore's Room, The Tavern, and Waterside Patio & Bar. The chowder, of

course, is available in all locations. They will ship their chowder anywhere so you can enjoy a taste of Newport no matter where you live. Online reviews rave about this chowder, proclaiming it "the best in the world." The award-winning chowder is also available by the can or the case through the Only in Rhode Island retail store located at The Shops at Long Wharf Mall in Newport and through their website (onlyinrhodeisland.com).

The Mayor's Own Marinara Sauce

buddycianci.com

"Real Italian-Style Sauce with Old World Charm"—so reads the label on jars of Buddy Cianci's marinara sauce.

Cianci was mayor of Providence for decades before being convicted on racketeering charges and sent to prison. Having done his time, Cianci is now a popular radio show host in Rhode Island. Throughout all his ups and downs, Cianci has been selling his jars of sauce in supermarkets and gourmet shops across the state. Fans describe it as "bright, fresh, and tomatoey." Proceeds from the sale of the sauce go to a scholarship fund, which has helped more than a hundred Providence children go to college.

Coffee Syrup: Autocrat vs. Dave's

Coffee milk is the official state drink of Rhode Island. For more than one hundred years, coffee milk lovers have been using Autocrat coffee syrup (autocrat.com), produced in Lincoln. Simply mix two tablespoons of coffee syrup with seven ounces of cold milk. But there's so much more you can do with coffee syrup. Autocrat's website has a wonderful recipe section. A newcomer on the local coffee syrup scene is Dave's Coffee, a craft coffee roaster with headquarters in Charlestown (davescoffeestore.com), where you can visit their espresso bar and bakery. Which one is better? You'll have to conduct your own taste test to find out. Both products are available online and in supermarkets throughout the state.

Daniele Inc.

danielefoods.com

Some of the finest charcuterie in the world is made in Pascoag, a small village in Rhode Island, where Daniele Inc. is located. It all started more than thirty years ago when the Dukcevich family brought their *salumi* to America from northern Italy. Today their hogs are raised on family farms in America. The pork is dry cured for months using basic ingredients and ancient methods. The results include superb prosciutto, soppressata, salami, capocollo, pancetta, mortadella, and chorizo. Daniele products are sold in supermarkets throughout the region, and the company's online storefront can be found on amazon.com.

Del's Frozen Lemonade

dels.com

It began in Italy in 1840 when great-grandfather DeLucia combined mountain snow, fresh lemon juice, and just the right amount of sugar to make lemon ice to sell at the local market. Around 1900 Grandfather Franco DeLucia brought the family's recipe for frozen lemonade to America. His son Angelo created a machine to produce a consistently excellent product. In 1948, Del's Lemonade opened a stand in Cranston, Rhode Island, and soon mobile units were on the road selling frozen lemonade throughout the state. His son Bruce has brought the flourishing business into the new millennium, and Bruce's daughter Stephanie is now in the business. Del's is definitely a family affair. You know it's spring in Rhode Island when Del's opens for the season and the bright green and yellow trucks pop up here and there. There is nothing quite as refreshing as an all-natural Del's Frozen Lemonade.

Fortuna Sausage Company

fortunasausage.com

Like so many other cottage industries, this business started more than one hundred years ago when a married couple immigrated to the United States with hopes, dreams, and some great Italian recipes. Today the third generation of the Fortuna family continues the tradition, offering quality sausages and Italian specialties in select markets and online. Their most famous product is known as Soupy, a Calabrese-style salami. All natural, nitrate-free, dry cured and dense, Soupy is offered with different levels of heat, from Sweet to Nuclear Hot. Each stick of Soupy is handmade, from the trimming of the pork and stuffing the family recipe into natural casings to hand tying each sausage with cotton twine and hanging it to air dry for eight to ten weeks—a dying tradition. Soupy can be sliced and eaten in sandwiches, salads, or alone as a snack.

Kenyon's Grist Mill

kenyonsgristmill.com

The quaintest corner of Rhode Island has to be Usque-paugh, where Kenyon's Grist Mill is located on the banks of the Queen's River. Since 1696, they have been grinding whole kernels of corn and whole berries of grain into meals and flours with huge granite millstones. Their most popular products, available in supermarkets and online, are the mixes that make clam cakes, pancakes, corn bread, muffins, brown bread, and johnny-cakes. Kenyon's shop is open year-round and well worth a visit, especially on a crisp fall day when the trees are ablaze with color. Old-fashioned events there include the annual Johnny Cake Festival in October.

Narragansett Creamery

richeeses.com

Award-winning artisan cheeses are made in Providence, Rhode Island, thanks to Narragansett Creamery, which is run by the Federico family. In 2007, Mark and Pattie Federico launched the artisan division of their umbrella company, Providence Specialty Products. Within a few years, their cheeses became a regular part of the culinary scene in southern New England, from their smoked mozzarella and Salty Sea Feta to their Renaissance Ricotta and Queso Blanco. Their products are available online, in stores throughout the state, and on the menus of nearly a hundred restaurants.

Newport Creamery

newportcreamery.com

It's awful big and awful good—that's why they call it the Awful Awful, the popular signature drink of Newport Creamery, a small chain of family restaurants now with thirteen locations based in Rhode Island. The Awful Awful is an ice cream–based beverage also known as a cabinet or frappe. It comes in six flavors: strawberry, vanilla, chocolate, chocolate mint, mocha, and coffee, the most popular. Known for its "good mood food," Newport Creamery got its start in 1928 as a milk business run by the Rector family, delivering house to house in the Newport area. With the opening of its first store in 1940 in Middletown, the Rectors started selling ice cream, and the Awful Awful  was trademarked in 1948. Today Newport Creamery is owned by the Jan Companies, and it continues to be a favorite spot for Rhode Island families to dine.

Olneyville New York System

olneyvillenewyorksystem.com

For more than sixty years, the Stevens family has operated the Olneyville New York System, a lunch counter serving natural casing wieners topped with a special meat sauce, mustard, onions, and celery salt on a steamed bun. You can buy the secret spice mix online and in supermarkets so you can make that special meat sauce at home. Step-by-step directions can be found on the website. There are two locations: 20 Plainfield Street in the Olneyville section of Providence, and 1012 Reservoir Avenue in Cranston. Both spots are open from lunch on into the wee hours of the next morning. Olneyville New York System wieners are considered by many to be Rhode Island's favorite fast food.

Yacht Club Soda

yachtclubsoda.com

Family owned and operated, Yacht Club Bottling Works opened in 1915 with the goal of bringing premium quality beverages to Rhode Island. Yacht Club is now considered the state's official soda. All its carbonated drinks are in glass bottles, which are returnable and reused, keeping more than 120,000 bottles out of local landfills annually. Yacht Club soda starts with water from an artesian well drilled through bedrock 180 feet below the bottling building. The natural mineral water has a temperature of forty-five degrees, which allows carbonation without the use of cooling towers that can be bad for the environment. The company also makes syrups on site with only pure cane sugar mixed with the artesian water (sugar-free options are also available). Devotees love Yacht Club's clean and smooth flavor.

JAMESTOWN FISH

14 NARRAGANSETT AVENUE
JAMESTOWN, RI 02835
(401) 423-FISH
JAMESTOWNFISHRI.COM
EXECUTIVE CHEF MATTHEW MACCARTNEY

Picture perfect—that best describes Jamestown Fish and the extraordinary food that is served within this stylish restaurant. Jamestown is the quintessential seaside village, a quaint harbor town with a solid number of very good restaurants. Jamestown Fish is the new kid on the block, so to speak, and it is already one of the finest restaurants not only in Jamestown but in the entire state.

Executive Chef Matthew MacCartney is also a partner at Jamestown Fish, owned by two of his biggest fans, Cathy and John Recca. While the Reccas are the first to appreciate the aromatic scents and artful presentations coming from Chef MacCartney's kitchen, they are also quick to note that more importantly his food is quite delicious. If you're looking for pretentious cuisine, you'll have to go elsewhere. The entire team at Jamestown Fish is committed to truly wonderful food and sincere service to match.

Jamestown Fish is housed in what appears to be a very well maintained seaside cottage. Inside, the ocean-blue walls are set off by crisp white trim. The dining room sparkles in the sunlight, which Sunday brunch guests get to experience. This restaurant is open just for dinner the rest of the week, with sunsets giving the dining room a warm

glow. Certain tables offer a view of the sailboats in Jamestown Harbor. Other popular spots are the tables for two near the fireplace and the handful of seats at a handsome bar. Upstairs is the Bridge Bar with a deck that offers a view of the Newport Bridge. In warm weather, outdoor dining is available on the patio where gourmet pizza is created in a beautiful pizza oven. Hours of operation fluctuate with the seasons so it's wise to always check the restaurant's website.

The menu is seasonal as well, but there's one dish you can always count on—the restaurant's famous fish soup, a spicy blend of the daily catch flavored with tomato, saffron, and fennel, served with a crisp wafer of cooked gruyère cheese. The mostly seafood menu is not your usual clam shack fare. Daurade is European sea bream roasted and served whole with Grenobloise sauce. The yellowfin tuna is coated in fresh herbs, seared on the *plancha* (Spanish for griddle), and served rare with celeriac puree. A pan-seared beef rib eye with dauphinoise potatoes is sure to satisfy any landlubber.

All this and more is the masterful work of Chef MacCartney and his talented team. With more than twenty years in the business, the chef has worked at some of New York's finest establishments, including Restaurant Daniel, Gramercy Tavern, and Craft. Early in his career, he worked in a Michelin three-star restaurant in France and at the world-renowned Cibreo in Florence, Italy. Before coming to Rhode Island, Chef MacCartney was at Pasta Nostra in Connecticut, regarded by many as one of the best Italian restaurants in the country. His sous chef there was Heliovaldo Araujo, who now works as the sous chef at Jamestown Fish. Together, they are an unbeatable team.

Jamestown Fish Soup

(MAKES 1 QUART OR 4 SERVINGS)

½ onion, chopped

¼ fennel, sliced

Olive oil, as needed

1 garlic clove, minced

¼ teaspoon saffron

¼ teaspoon oregano

¼ teaspoon fennel seed

¼ cup Pernod

¼ cup cream sherry

¼ cup tomato paste

3 anchovies

8 ounces monkfish

8 ounces cod

1 quart plus 1 cup fish stock

Extra-virgin olive oil, as needed for garnish

In a stockpot, sweat the onions and fennel in a little olive oil until they are translucent. Add the garlic and spices, and cook for 1 minute. Add the Pernod and sherry, and mix well. Add the tomato paste and anchovies, and mix well. Add the fish and fish stock, and mix well. Simmer for 15 minutes.

Using a hand blender or an immersion blender, puree until smooth.

Pour the fish soup into warm serving bowls. Drizzle with extra virgin olive oil just before serving.

Big Eye Tuna
with Herbs & Green Olive Tapenade

(SERVES 4)

Chef MacCartney's note: At our restaurant, the tuna is rolled in herbs and seared rare on the *plancha* (Spanish for griddle). Home cooks can duplicate this cooking method by using an electric griddle, the kind used to make pancakes, inexpensive and readily available. The garnish is fennel, red peppers, and olive tapenade. Tapenade is a condiment from southern France usually made of pureed olives, capers, garlic, anchovies, lemon, parsley, and olive oil.

For the tapenade:

2 small garlic cloves
¼ cup Castelvetrano olives (pitted)
2 anchovy fillets
¼ cup chopped parsley
1 tablespoon lemon juice
1 tablespoon capers
¼ cup extra-virgin olive oil

For the side vegetables:

1 fennel bulb
2 red peppers
Olive oil, as needed
1 garlic clove, sliced
Salt, to taste

For the tuna:

1 cup parsley, stems removed but the leaves left whole
1 cup cilantro, stems removed but the leaves left whole
1 tablespoon cumin
1 tablespoon black pepper
1 tablespoon hot pepper flakes
4 equal portions sushi-grade tuna, 8 ounces each
1 tablespoon salt

To make the tapenade: Place the garlic cloves in a food processor and pulse until finely chopped. Add the remaining tapenade ingredients except the olive oil. Puree the mixture. When the mixture is coarsely chopped, slowly add the olive oil. Set aside.

To make the side vegetables: Slice the fennel and peppers lengthwise into ⅓-inch strips. Over low heat in a frying pan, heat a little olive oil and the garlic. Cook the garlic until light golden brown in color, then remove the garlic and add the fennel and peppers. Season with salt. Sweat the vegetables until they are soft but not mushy.

To make the tuna: Wash and dry the parsley and cilantro, and pick the leaves off the stems. Chop the parsley and cilantro medium fine with a very sharp knife, which helps retain the green color by not bruising the herbs. Add the spices and reserve the mixture on a plate.

Coat the tuna with the herb mixture and salt one side of the tuna steaks. Add a little olive oil to the griddle and place the salted side of the tuna down first. Season the top side of the tuna with salt. Cook for 1 minute on each side, and remove the tuna from the griddle. The tuna should be rare. Slice the tuna on a bias.

To plate: Mound the warm fennel and pepper mixture in the center of each dinner plate, and place the tuna on top. Spread 1 tablespoon of tapenade on the plate around the tuna.

Chef MacCartney's note: If you wish, add a touch of flaky sea salt, a drizzle of your best olive oil, and a dusting of fennel pollen (available at gourmet markets).

For such a small island, Block Island has an extraordinary number of excellent restaurants. Just over a thousand people live on the island year-round, and they are the lucky ones who are able to dine in the off-season at Aldo's Italian Restaurant, Sharky's, and Dead Eye Dick's (a great place to watch the sunset). The Hotel Manisses Restaurant is elegant and intimate. The Spring House offers high-end cuisine in three separate venues. At the Sunset Bistro, you just might bump into actor Christopher Walken, who owns a house on Block Island.

The quintessential dining experience on Block Island is the shore dinner served at Ballard's (42 Water Street, 401-466-2231, ballardsinn.com). Native steamers (about two pounds per person) are served first along with warm cups of golden clarified butter. Ballard's famous quahog chowder is next with its chopped clams and a hint of fresh thyme. Many people also opt for the mussels marinara with the heady flavors of garlic, oregano, and white wine. This is all leading up to the main event: a boiled lobster weighing at least 1¼ pounds, with more drawn butter for dipping. Steaming ears of corn, red skin potatoes, and perhaps even some chorizo round out the menu with watermelon, of course, for dessert.

A traditional shore dinner is timeless. Perfection on a plate (or on a series of plates), this is how they've been doing it for decades on Block Island.

PLUM POINT BISTRO

1814 BOSTON NECK ROAD
SAUNDERSTOWN, RI 02874
(401) 667-4999
PLUMPTBISTRO.COM
EXECUTIVE CHEF RALPH CONTE

Ralph Conte is one of those important Rhode Island chefs who helped elevate the state's culinary reputation with the progressive Italian food he served at his Providence restaurants back in the 1990s. He has now evolved into a suburban restaurant owner with his wife, Elisa, and two grown children by his side at Plum Point Bistro. All are involved in the business.

From opening day in 2012, this seaside bistro has attracted capacity crowds consisting of Ralph's fans from his Providence days to new admirers who have fallen in

love with his new French-Italian menu. That one-page seasonal menu offers appetizers such as shrimp bruschetta and purses filled with the tender meat from a short rib. Pork chops are done up alla parmigiana or paired with maple bacon red cabbage. Not surprisingly, pasta plays a major role, with Conte updating standard Italian dishes.

And you might want to know that striped bass you're dining on was swimming that morning in local waters. Ralph Conte is an avid fisherman and often brings in that day's catch to his busy restaurant.

Thanks to a stylish tin ceiling, the noise level at Plum Point Bistro can be loud, especially when it's packed with high-energy clientele. But that defines a true bistro—an informal, boisterous gathering place, a hot trend in restaurants today. A huge blackboard listing the nightly specials hangs on the back wall. Other design elements include a wall of wine bottles that separates the bar and lounge area from the dining room. Leather-bound books and eclectic artwork help set a mood that transports guests from little Rhode Island to somewhere in Europe. In actuality, Plum Point is centrally located between quaint Jamestown, affluent East Greenwich, and the beaches of Narragansett.

Ditalini with Escarole, Beans & Sausage

(SERVES 4)

¼ cup extra-virgin olive oil, divided
7 garlic cloves, peeled, divided
1 onion, diced
1 head escarole, washed and cut into 2-inch wide strips
1 pound Italian sausage, casings removed and
    crumbled
2 cups chicken broth
1 (16-ounce) can cannellini beans, drained and rinsed
1 teaspoon crushed red pepper
1 teaspoon freshly ground black pepper
Salt, to taste
1 cup ditalini pasta
4 slices rustic bread

In a large pot, heat 2 tablespoons of the oil over medium heat. Slice 6 of the garlic cloves and add them to the pot. Add the onion. Cook until translucent, about 5 minutes. Be careful not to burn the garlic.

Fold in the escarole and sausage. Sauté until the escarole starts to wilt, about 5 minutes. Pour in the broth. Simmer for 30 minutes, stirring occasionally to prevent sticking.

Add the beans, red pepper, black pepper, and salt. Simmer another 20 minutes, stirring occasionally. Stir in the pasta and cook for another 10 minutes.

Meanwhile, toast the bread until it is a golden brown. Rub the toasted bread with the remaining garlic clove.

When done, this dish should resemble a stew more than a soup. Drizzle with the remaining olive oil. Serve hot accompanied by the garlic-rubbed toasted bread.

Linguine in Clam Sauce with Summer Tomatoes

(SERVES 4)

24 littleneck clams
Salt, as needed
½ cup extra-virgin olive oil, divided
12 garlic cloves, sliced
4 ripe tomatoes, cut into ¼-inch cubes
1 cup dry white wine
Freshly ground black pepper, to taste
12 fresh oregano sprigs, leaves only, chopped
1 pound linguine
1 bunch basil, leaves only, cut into julienne strips

Place the clams in a large bowl. Add enough water to cover the clams. Pour in 1 tablespoon of salt. Set aside to soak for 30 minutes. Drain and rinse under cold running water to remove any sand in the clams.

Heat ⅓ cup of the oil in a large sauté pan. Add the garlic and clams. Cook over medium heat until the garlic starts to brown, about 1 minute. Stir in the tomatoes, wine, pepper, and oregano. Cover and simmer for 10 minutes, or until the clams open. Discard any unopened clams.

Bring 5 quarts of salted water to a boil in a large pot. Add the linguine. Cook until al dente. Drain the pasta. Toss the cooked linguine with the clam sauce. Season with salt, if needed. Fold in the basil. Serve the linguine in a very large heated bowl, drizzled with the remaining olive oil.

IN THE
SUBURBS

Avenue N American Kitchen

20 Newman Avenue
Rumford, RI 02916
(401) 270-AVEN
AVENUENAMERICANKITCHEN.COM
Executive Chef Nick Rabar

From the day that Avenue N American Kitchen opened its doors in 2010, this stylish restaurant has been packed with customers, many of them now "regulars" who dine there several times every week. What draws people back again and again is Chef-Owner Nick Rabar's honest food with wife and business partner Tracy Rabar ensuring a warm and friendly atmosphere.

Local fans have been tracking Chef Rabar's career for more than a decade as he climbed the culinary ladder that brought him to his ultimate destination—owning his own restaurant. The Rabars decided to open in their hometown of Rumford, where Avenue N has become a suburban oasis. Their contemporary bistro is located in an old building with deep industrial roots. In the 1800s, it was the home of the Rumford Chemical Works, makers of the now-famous Rumford Baking Powder. Chef Rabar utilizes that tried-and-true brand of baking powder in several of his recipes. Similarly, Avenue N utilizes the raw elements of the historic building for its interior design—polished concrete, exposed brick, wood beams, and industrial ductwork. In warm weather, dinner is also served on a beautiful brick patio.

In direct contrast, Chef Rabar's food is thoroughly modern. Local and seasonal ingredients are used to prepare delicious, creative fare such as barbecue duck sliders, malt-glazed chicken wings, and a braised all-natural beef short rib served with cheddar cheese and green onion grits. The playful side of his menu offers hand-battered corn dogs with mac and cheese on the side as an appetizer.

"I want to offer guests the kind of food and hospitality that brings to mind the comforts of home," said the award-winning chef.

When Chef Rabar isn't in the kitchen, he can be found right next door at The Pantry, a local market concept offering prepared foods such as chickpea and chorizo bisque, buttermilk fried chicken, and polenta cakes stuffed with ham and gruyère cheese. He's also the host of a local lifestyle/cooking show, Chef 2 Go. Somehow Chef Rabar has even found time to write his first novel, *The Cold Side of the Grill*.

Pan-Roasted Chicken with Amish Corn & Hen of the Woods Mushrooms

(SERVES 4)

For the chicken:

4 bone-in all-natural chicken breasts,
  with skin left on
1 large rosemary sprig
2 tablespoons olive oil
1 tablespoon kosher salt
½ teaspoon cracked black pepper
Zest and juice from 1 lemon

For the Amish corn:

½ Vidalia onion, cut into small dice
3 ears of corn, shucked, with the kernels
  removed from the cob
1 cup cream
¼ cup sugar
1 tablespoon salt

For the celeriac-potato puree:

1 head celeriac, peeled, cut into large dice
2 Idaho potatoes, peeled, cut into large dice
1½ tablespoons salt
6 tablespoons butter
¼ cup heavy cream

For the pancetta-Madeira jus:

2 ounces pancetta
1 cup Madeira wine
2 small hen of the woods mushrooms
2 cups veal glacé or rich stock
1 pinch chopped rosemary

To make the chicken: Preheat oven to 450°F.

In a sealed plastic bag or plastic container with
a lid, combine the chicken with the rosemary,
olive oil, salt, pepper, lemon zest, and some of
the lemon juice to marinate for at least 24 hours.
In an ovenproof frying pan, pan-sear the chicken
breasts over medium-high heat, skin side down,
until golden brown. Turn the breasts over, and
place the frying pan in a preheated 450°F oven
for 15 minutes, or until done.

To make the Amish corn: In a 4-quart saucepan,
lightly sauté the onions, but do not brown. Add
the corn, cream, sugar, and salt. Cook over low
heat for 30 minutes, or until the corn is softened.

To make the celeriac-potato puree: In another 4-quart saucepan, cover the celeriac and potatoes with cold water. Add the salt. Bring to a boil, and cook until fork tender, about 20 minutes. Drain well. Mash with the butter and cream. Salt to taste.

To make the jus: Sauté the pancetta until crispy. Deglaze the pan with Madeira wine, and reduce by half. Add the mushrooms, veal glacé or stock, and chopped rosemary. Reduce again by half or until it coats the back of a spoon.

To plate: Place a chicken breast over a serving of the celeriac-potato puree and some of the Amish corn. Drizzle the jus over the chicken breast.

CHICKEN DUMPLING & RUMFORD BISCUIT SOUP
(SERVES 5)

For the soup:

2 carrots, peeled and cut into medium dice
1 onion, cut into medium dice
2 celery stalks, cut into medium dice
2 parsnips, peeled and cut into medium dice
¼ celery root, peeled and cut into medium dice
1 tablespoon olive oil
2 quarts chicken stock
4 thyme sprigs
4 bay leaves
2 tablespoons tomato paste
¼ cup white wine
2 tablespoons kosher salt
¼ teaspoon black pepper
1 cup grated Romano cheese

For the dumplings: (Makes 20 dumplings)

1 pound ground chicken
½ cup panko bread crumbs
¼ cup grated Romano cheese
1 tablespoon olive oil
½ small shallot, minced
1 teaspoon chopped rosemary
½ teaspoon chopped thyme

1 pinch paprika
1 pinch garlic powder
1 pinch salt
1 pinch black pepper

For the biscuits: (Makes 10 biscuits)

2 cups all-purpose flour
3 teaspoons Rumford baking powder
1 teaspoon kosher salt
6 tablespoons melted butter
⅔ cup buttermilk

To make the soup: In a stockpot, sauté the diced carrots, onions, celery, parsnips, and celery root in the oil. Cook until softened, but do not brown. Add the chicken stock, thyme, bay leaves, tomato paste, white wine, salt, and pepper. Simmer for 30 minutes over low heat. Fold in the Romano cheese prior to serving. Makes ½ gallon, or eight (8-ounce) servings.

To make the dumplings: Preheat oven to 450°F. In a large bowl, combine all the ingredients. Form into 20 tiny meatballs. Place the meatballs in a baking pan. Bake for approximately 10 minutes.

To make the biscuits: Preheat oven to 350°F. In a large bowl, combine all the ingredients and mix well to make a dough. Cut the dough into 10 equal pieces. Form the biscuits. Bake for 10–12 minutes, or until golden brown.

To serve: Ladle some of the soup into a deep soup bowl. Add four or five meatballs to each bowl of soup. Top each serving with two buttermilk biscuits. Serve immediately.

BLACKIE'S BULLDOG TAVERN

181 GEORGE WASHINGTON HIGHWAY
SMITHFIELD, RI 02917
(401) 231-4777
BLACKIESBULLDOGTAVERN.COM
EXECUTIVE CHEF ANGIE ARMENISE

I LOVE YOU MORE THAN BACON. That's just one of the fun signs hanging in Blackie's Bulldog Tavern, where Executive Chef Angie Armenise is creating wildly wonderful food, often topped with bacon.

Take her "American as Apple Pie" Burger, the most popular item on her expansive menu. A juicy nine-ounce burger is cooked to your specifications, then topped with crisp

bacon, sharp cheddar cheese, brown sugar-maple mayonnaise, and finally a warm apple-pear compote (with fruit from local farms, of course). These layers of flavor are tucked carefully into a buttery pretzel roll for one of the most interesting burgers on earth. And that's just one of the talented chef's many original creations.

You'll need two hands to handle the creative burgers, sandwiches, and wraps on the menu, which also offers plenty of unique appetizers (I recommend the Buffalo Dip), salads with house-made dressings, rustic flatbreads, and hearty entrees. Modern-day comfort food is the house specialty, from the amazing grilled salmon BLT to cheddar and mushroom meatloaf. And you can't go wrong with any dish that contains Chef Armenise's famous short ribs. For example, her shepherd's pie combines garlic mashed potatoes and corn with the braised and pulled meat from beef short ribs. That same tender meat stars in the short rib pappardelle dish with a rich fig gravy and a spritz of truffle oil. Many menu items are also available as gluten-free dishes.

This is all from a very special chef who has been gathering fans for the past decade as she worked in Providence restaurants before moving to the suburbs to become the chef and a co-owner of Blackie's with General Manager Jeanine Iannucci. With a bachelor's degree in culinary arts from Johnson & Wales University, Chef Angie has also worked at restaurants in Chicago and Ireland. Part of her mission in life is to give back to the community, and the award-winning chef volunteers her time with a great number of organizations.

The interior of Blackie's has a sleek black and chartreuse color scheme with amusing modern art on the walls. The restaurant's motto is: "Eat or be eaten." With a fun attitude like that, it's no surprise that Blackie's is packed with happy customers just about every night of the week.

Short Rib Pappardelle

(SERVES 4)

2 pounds boneless beef short ribs

Salt and pepper, to taste

1 tablespoon olive oil

2 large carrots

4 celery stalks

4 garlic cloves

1 medium-size Vidalia onion

1 tablespoon whole black peppercorns

4 bay leaves

1 gallon beef stock

1 cup dry red wine

4 ounces caramelized onions

1 cup beef demi-glacé (make your own or buy premade at gourmet markets)

2 tablespoons fig jam

½ cup heavy cream

½ cup shaved Parmigiano-Reggiano cheese

24 ounces pappardelle pasta (black pepper–flavored is recommended)

6 ounces goat cheese

1 tablespoon freshly minced chives

1 teaspoon white truffle oil

Whole chives, for garnish

Season the short ribs liberally with salt and pepper, and sear them on all sides in batches in the oil in a large sauté pan over high heat. Once browned nicely on all sides, place the ribs in a large casserole dish or roasting pan.

Preheat oven to 350°F.

Wash, peel, rough chop, and place the carrots, celery, garlic, and onions around the ribs. Add the peppercorns, bay leaves, beef stock, and red wine. Cover the roasting pan with foil. Place the pan in the 350°F oven for approximately 3–5 hours or until the meat falls apart when touched with a fork.

Remove the ribs from the pan and allow to cool enough so that you can shred the meat with your hands. Place the shredded meat in a saucepan with the caramelized onions, beef demi-glacé, fig jam, cream, and Parmigiano-Reggiano cheese. Cook over low heat until the cheese is melted.

Cook the pasta to al dente, drain, and mix with the warmed sauce.

In a small bowl, mix the goat cheese with the minced chives, truffle oil, and salt and pepper to taste.

To serve, place a portion of the pasta-meat mixture into a warm deep bowl, making sure to divide the sauce evenly. Spoon a tablespoon or so of the goat cheese mixture on top of the hot pasta. Garnish with a whole chive and serve immediately.

Apple-Pear Compote

(SERVES 4)

Chef Angie's note: This apple-pear compote is an essential part of one of the most popular items on our menu, the "American as Apple Pie" burger. A 9-ounce burger is placed inside a buttery pretzel roll that has been smeared with brown sugar-maple mayonnaise. The burger is topped with sharp cheddar cheese, crisp bacon, and onion rings, and on top of all that, our apple-pear compote—for a burger unlike any other you've ever had.

For the compote:

2 tablespoons unsalted butter
2 Granny Smith apples, peeled and diced
2 Red Delicious apples, peeled and diced
2 pears, peeled and diced
¼ cup brown sugar
¼ cup dried cherries
¼ cup cinnamon simple syrup (recipe follows)
1 teaspoon vanilla extract
1 teaspoon almond extract
1 teaspoon ground cinnamon
Juice and zest from 1 lemon

For the cinnamon simple syrup:

2 parts sugar to 1 part water
1 cinnamon stick

To make the compote: In a large sauté pan over medium-low heat, melt the butter. Add the apples and pears. Cook over low heat until the apples begin to soften.

Add the brown sugar, dried cherries, simple syrup, extracts, and ground cinnamon. Add the lemon juice and zest. Mix well. Move the mixture from the sauté pan into a large enough storage container and allow to cool.

To make the cinnamon simple syrup: In a saucepan, combine the sugar and water over medium heat. Stir constantly until the sugar is completely dissolved. Bring to a boil. Reduce to a simmer. Add the cinnamon stick to impart flavor while the syrup is simmering. Remove the pan from the heat. Allow the syrup to cool completely and thicken before use.

Chef Angie's note: You can make as small or as large a batch of the cinnamon simple syrup as you desire. Make extra syrup and store it in your refrigerator. It will keep in the refrigerator for 6 months. You can use it in a number of ways, including in your favorite hot or cold beverages.

BOAT HOUSE

227 SCHOONER DRIVE
TIVERTON, RI 02878
(401) 624-6300
BOATHOUSETIVERTON.COM
EXECUTIVE CHEF JULIO LAZZARINI

When it comes to majestic water views, it's hard to beat the 180-degree panorama offered at the Boat House on the banks of the Sakonnet River. This handsome restaurant started out as an open-air summer watering hole that was so popular and so successful that the decision was made to enclose the seasonal business and turn it into a year-round dining destination. More than ever, it is now one of the state's most appealing restaurants.

Owned and operated by the prestigious Newport Restaurant Group, the Boat House has legions of fans who dine there regularly. The eighteen-seat granite-topped bar draws a friendly crowd from lunch on through the evening hours. A sturdy pier extends out into the water, enabling boaters to stop in for a bite to eat in warm weather. They feel right at home with the nautical decor—oars serve as part of the interior design, along with oversized seafood art prints, and charts depicting the colorful flag signals used by yachtsmen. From the soaring ceiling hang antique black iron chandeliers and ceiling fans that lend a tropical touch to the spacious restaurant.

Preparing beautiful food for this beautiful setting is Executive Chef Julio Lazzarini, who was born in Puerto Rico. Before coming to the Boat House, he was the chef-owner of a restaurant in Wilmington, Delaware. His current menu overflows with seafood delicacies, from lobster fritters with chipotle aioli to pan-roasted sole with tomato relish. This modern-day "seafood shack" has an impeccable raw bar featuring native oysters, littlenecks, and shrimp cocktail. The award-winning chowder has just a touch of chorizo. Beyond the sea, the chef offers grilled pork chops, Hereford beef steaks, and chicken with imaginative accompaniments such as succotash and creamed spinach. Vegetarian and gluten-free menus are also available.

In its very peaceful setting, the Boat House is one of the best restaurants in the state to watch the sunset any time of the year.

Pan-Roasted Sole with Rice Pilaf, Tomato Relish & Citrus Beurre Blanc

(SERVES 4)

For the rice pilaf:

Up to 4 cups chicken or vegetable stock (amount
    depends on the type of rice used)
2 teaspoons chicken fat or olive oil
2 cups white rice (preferably long grain)
½ cup chopped yellow onions
½ cup chopped celery
2 teaspoons kosher salt
¼ teaspoon ground black pepper
½ cup chopped fresh parsley

For the tomato relish:

½ cup lime juice
½ cup white wine vinegar
½ cup chopped cilantro
½ cup chopped Italian parsley
1 cup olive oil
7 tablespoons chopped fresh garlic
⅓ cup chopped jalapeños
1 small diced yellow bell pepper
1 small diced red bell pepper
4 scallions, chopped
2 pounds cherry tomatoes, halved
Salt and black pepper, to taste

For the citrus beurre blanc:

½ cup dry white wine
½ cup orange juice, freshly squeezed
¼ cup lemon juice, freshly squeezed
¼ cup lime juice, freshly squeezed
¼ cup thinly sliced shallots
1 (2-inch) strip orange zest
1 (2-inch) strip lemon zest
1 (2-inch) strip lime zest

1 garlic clove, smashed
½ bay leaf
1 thyme sprig
½ teaspoon salt
½ teaspoon black peppercorns
⅓ cup heavy cream
½ pound cold unsalted butter, cut into cubes

For the sole:

4 sole fillets
Salt and pepper, to taste
2 tablespoons unsalted butter
Canola oil, as needed for sautéing

To make the rice pilaf: Heat the correct amount
of stock needed in a large saucepan (at least a
2-quart size saucepan).

Chef Julio's note: You want to cook the rice in
a liquid that is primarily stock—either chicken
stock or vegetable stock. At least half of the liquid
should be stock, and the rest can be plain water.

While the stock is heating, heat a large skillet
over medium high heat. Add the chicken fat (or
oil), melting it so it coats the bottom of the pan.
Add the uncooked rice, stirring occasionally, for
a couple of minutes. Add the onions and celery
and cook a few minutes longer, until the onions
begin to soften.

If you are using canned or boxed stock, be
careful how much seasoning you add. If you are
starting with a seasoned stock, you may only
need to add a teaspoon of kosher salt. Taste the
stock. It can be a little on the salty side because
the rice will absorb a lot of the salt.

Carefully combine the rice mixture into the saucepan with the stock. Bring to a simmer, reduce the heat, cover, and cook for 15–25 minutes. (Use a timer.) At no point during the cooking of the rice should you uncover the pan. Remove the pan from the heat and let sit for 10 minutes, covered. Fluff with a fork to serve. Season to taste with salt and pepper. Stir in the chopped parsley.

To make the tomato relish: In a large bowl, mix all the ingredients together. Season with salt and pepper. Refrigerate until you are ready to serve.

To make the citrus beurre blanc: Place all the ingredients except the heavy cream and butter in a 1-quart saucepan over high heat. Bring to a boil and reduce until the liquid is nearly evaporated, 12–14 minutes. Add the heavy cream to the pan and reduce by half, 3–6 minutes.

Remove the pan from the heat and reduce the temperature to medium-low.

Add a few cubes of the butter to the pan, using a whisk to stir constantly until the butter is melted.

Return the pan to the heat and add a few more cubes of butter. Continue to place the pan on and off the heat, adding a few cubes of butter to the pan and whisking, until all the butter is used.

Remove the sauce from the heat and strain through a fine-mesh strainer. Keep warm until ready to serve. Do not allow the sauce to boil or it will separate.

To make the sole: With a knife, remove the skin from the sole fillets, leaving only the white flesh of the fish. Season each fillet on both sides with salt and pepper. In a large sauté pan, heat the butter and just enough canola oil to cover the bottom of the pan over high heat. Place the sole fillets in the pan, and sear both sides until they are slightly brown and cooked through.

To plate: Place a serving of the rice pilaf in the center of each dinner plate. Top the rice with the cooked sole. Garnish with the tomato relish. Drizzle the citrus beurre blanc lightly over the entire dish.

Chapel Grille

3000 Chapel View Boulevard
Cranston, RI 02920
(401) 944-4900
chapelgrilleri.com
Executive Chef Tim Kelly
Pastry Chef Erin Farrar

Restaurants are a very popular topic of conversation in Rhode Island. "Guess who's opened a new restaurant? Have you been there yet? I hear it's wonderful." Food seems to be our common language, whether you're from Westerly or Woonsocket. For years, people heard rumors of a fabulous new restaurant coming to Cranston. When it became official, food lovers watched the painstaking progress that led to the opening of Chapel Grille, which remains one of the most talked about restaurants in the state.

Part of this restaurant's mystique is its executive chef, Tim Kelly, who for years had been the chef at the well-respected Cafe Nuovo in Providence. Always dressed in spotless chef whites, Kelly often visits with dinner guests to make certain they are satisfied. It's that attention to detail that makes this stunning restaurant so special.

Located within a village of trendy shops, Chapel Grille is quite impressive. The main building really was a chapel back in the 1800s, and it was renovated and expanded to resemble an English manor with beautiful stained glass windows. Lunch, dinner, and Sunday brunch are served in various rooms including the Conservatory and a glassed-in sky-view terrace. If you're there for brunch, try the bananas Foster pancakes, created by Pastry Chef Erin Farrar.

The restaurant's Mediterranean hearth–style cuisine is equally impressive. The ambitious menu focuses on the olive-growing regions of the world with many ingredients locally sourced. For starters, you can enjoy a glass of wine at the curved Cathedral Bar and watch your authentic Margherita pizza baking in the Wood Stone hearth oven. The Cleopatra Salad will transport you safely to the Middle East. The fish chowder and the bouillabaisse can be traced back to Marseilles. Several dishes including salmon and duck breast are cooked on the *plancha,* a Spanish flat-top

griddle. One of Chef Kelly's specialties is the braised lamb shank served with Sicilian couscous and Moroccan spices. Other extraordinary accompaniments include olive oil mashed potatoes, Parmesan-crusted polenta, and garlicky spinach.

Chapel Grille is steeped in history. Gigantic portraits of the original landowners, Stuckely Westcott III and his wife, Priscilla, overlook the Cathedral Bar and open kitchen. One can't help but wonder what they would think of Chapel Grille, one of the most fabulous restaurants in the state of Rhode Island.

GOAT CHEESE–STUFFED SICILIAN OLIVES

(MAKES 2 CUPS)

¼ cup extra-virgin olive oil
1 garlic clove, roughly chopped
1 rosemary sprig, roughly chopped
1 lemon, thinly sliced
1 pint pitted Sicilian olives
1 (3-ounce) log goat cheese

To marinate the olives: Place the olive oil, garlic, rosemary, and sliced lemon in a small mixing bowl, and crush with the back of a wooden spoon to release the flavors. Add the olives and gently mix. Cover the bowl with plastic wrap. Refrigerate for up 3 days. Gently toss the olives several times a day.

To stuff the olives: Soften the goat cheese by placing it in a small bowl, and stir it with a wooden spoon. Place the goat cheese in a pastry bag fitted with a small star tip, then pipe the goat cheese into the hole of each olive. Store in the refrigerator for up to 2 weeks.

BRAISED LAMB SHANKS

(SERVES 4–6)

Chef Kelly's note: This dish should be prepared two days in advance, the first day for initial braising of the lamb shanks (which takes about 4 hours), and the second day finishing the shanks (which takes about 1 hour). This way you will be able to easily remove the fat that overnight will solidify on the top of the yummy braising liquid. Also, Israeli couscous may be substituted for the Sicilian variety.

5 pounds extra-large lamb shanks
Kosher salt, as needed
Freshly ground black pepper, as needed
¼ cup vegetable oil
1 (28-ounce) can whole peeled plum tomatoes
½ pound Sicilian couscous (also known as
　fregola sarda)
20 pitted Moroccan olives (about ¼ pound)
4 stem-on artichoke hearts
10 saffron threads
1 teaspoon smoked paprika
½ teaspoon ground cumin
⅛ teaspoon ground cinnamon
¼ cup chopped Italian parsley

Day 1: Preheat oven to 275°F.

Liberally season the lamb shanks with kosher salt and freshly ground black pepper. On the stovetop over medium-high heat, brown the seasoned lamb shanks in the oil in a sauté pan, then transfer them to an 8- to 10-quart Dutch oven or a large crockpot. (You can brown them one at a time if your pan is small.)

Crush the tomatoes by hand and add them to the Dutch oven, then add enough water to cover the lamb shanks, keeping the water about an inch from the top of the pot. Add a teaspoon of kosher salt and about 10 turns of the pepper mill. Cover the Dutch oven and place in the 275°F oven. (You may want to place a sheet pan under the Dutch oven to catch any liquid that may simmer over the top.)

Allow the lamb shanks to braise for about 3 hours, then check them. The cooking time will vary slightly, depending on the size of the shanks. When they are done (in 3–4 hours), the meat should be almost falling from the bone and will easily pull away with a fork. Remove the Dutch oven from the oven, let it cool to room temperature uncovered, then store it covered overnight in the refrigerator.

Day 2: Preheat oven to 300°F.

Remove the Dutch oven from the refrigerator and uncover. Remove and discard the fat that will have risen to the top and hardened over the cooked lamb shanks. Place the Dutch oven over low heat and gently bring to a simmer. Add the couscous, olives, artichoke hearts, and spices. Cover and place in the 300°F oven for 1 hour. Sprinkle with the chopped parsley and serve family style.

BANANAS FOSTER PANCAKES

(MAKES 16 PANCAKES)

Chef Erin's note: Make the Foster butter, sautéed bananas, and Chantilly cream in advance. You can soften your butter by using the defrost function in a microwave oven, or you can leave the butter out at room temperature for a couple of hours. To chill the bowl for making Chantilly cream, simply place the bowl in the freezer to chill.

For the Foster butter:

8 ounces (2 sticks) unsalted butter, softened
½ teaspoon vanilla extract
Pinch of salt
¾ cup light brown sugar

For the sautéed bananas:

4 large bananas, peeled and sliced ¼-inch thick
Foster butter
¼ cup Myers's Dark Rum
¼ cup 99 Bananas liqueur

For the Chantilly cream:

½ cup heavy cream
1 tablespoon confectioners' sugar
⅛ teaspoon vanilla extract

For the pancakes:

2½ cups all-purpose flour
½ cup granulated sugar
2 teaspoons baking powder
1 teaspoon baking soda
Pinch of salt
2 teaspoons ground cinnamon*
1 teaspoon ground ginger*
½ teaspoon ground nutmeg*
½ teaspoon ground allspice*
2 whole eggs

*Or substitute 4 teaspoons pumpkin pie spice for all the above spices.

2½ cups buttermilk
½ cup vegetable oil
Butter, as needed

Sautéed bananas (recipe follows)
Foster butter (recipe follows)
Chantilly cream (recipe follows)
Cinnamon powder and confectioners' sugar, for garnish

To make the Foster butter: In a small mixing bowl, thoroughly combine all ingredients.

To make the sautéed bananas: In a large sauté pan over medium-high heat, sauté the bananas in about ¼ of the Foster butter for a couple of minutes. Deglaze the pan with the two liquors. Be prepared for the pan to flame up, especially if cooking on a gas stove. Simmer for a couple of minutes to cook out the alcohol, then whisk in the remaining butter to complete the sauce.

To make the Chantilly cream: Combine all the ingredients in a small chilled mixing bowl, then whisk until firm peaks form.

To make the pancakes: Preheat an electric griddle or electric frying pan to 325°F.

Combine the flour, sugar, baking powder, baking soda, salt, and spices in a large bowl. Whisk to combine.

In another bowl, combine the eggs, buttermilk, and oil. Whisk to combine. Pour the liquid mixture into the dry mixture, and mix until just combined. Some small lumps will remain.

Lightly butter the griddle. Ladle some of the batter onto the hot griddle, gently spreading it into even circles. Cook until bubbles begin to set around the edges. Gently flip each pancake and cook until golden brown on both sides.

To plate: Stack four pancakes onto the middle of each plate. Top with sautéed bananas and a dollop of Chantilly cream. Garnish with cinnamon powder and dust with confectioners' sugar.

D. CARLO TRATTORIA

970 DOUGLAS PIKE
SMITHFIELD, RI 02917
(401) 349-4979
DCARLOTRATTORIA.NET
EXECUTIVE CHEF AARON THORPE

When dozens of restaurants were opening in Providence, D. Carlo Trattoria quietly made its debut in the suburb of Smithfield, just outside the capital city. This casual Italian restaurant was quickly embraced by local food lovers, and a successful neighborhood restaurant was born.

Owners Denis Thibeault and Carlo Slaughter had paid their restaurant business dues in the city. In their joint venture, they crafted an authentic trattoria with a wonderful warm ambience and true Italian cuisine from the various regions of Italy. Located in a busy shopping plaza, the well-designed restaurant has a comfortable atmosphere with big leather couches and oversize coffee tables in the lounge area. It's a couple of steps up to the twelve-seat bar, which gives guests a view of the entire dining area with its earth-

tone color scheme and soft lighting. Wooden wine crates are part of the decor, along with Italian liquor posters.

Executive Chef Aaron Thorpe has created a menu that keeps his customers coming back again and again. Classic Italian dishes are offered, such as fried risotto balls stuffed with prosciutto, peas, and mozzarella; grilled Tuscan sausage served over broccoli rabe; and veal parmesan over penne pasta in a marinara sauce. And then the talented chef gets creative. A braised pork shank is served with bacon-cheddar risotto, pan-seared sea scallops sit atop a sunchoke puree, and grilled swordfish comes with sweet potato hash.

The eight pasta dishes on the menu are eight more reasons to visit D. Carlo Trattoria. Penne with a vodka tomato cream sauce, baked four-cheese ravioli, and pappardelle Bolognese are just some of the tempting offerings.

Save room for dessert, from a traditional tiramisu to the warm chocolate budino cake garnished with candied orange zest.

PAN-SEARED SEA SCALLOPS WITH ASPARAGUS CRÈME

(SERVES 2)

½ cup cranberry beans, soaked in water overnight

For the asparagus crème: (Makes 2 cups)

1 tablespoon butter
1 garlic clove, crushed
1 shallot, thinly sliced
1 cup heavy cream
1 bunch asparagus, trimmed and cut into pieces (about 1 pound)
Salt and pepper, to taste

For the brown butter vinaigrette: (Makes 1 cup)

4 tablespoons butter
¼ cup sherry vinegar
1 tablespoon honey
½ cup canola oil
Salt and pepper, to taste

For the scallops:

10 large sea scallops
1 tablespoon olive oil
Salt and pepper, to taste
8 fingerling potatoes, cut in half lengthwise
¼ pound Serrano ham, diced
6 grape tomatoes, cut in half
2 small bunches mâche lettuce

Start by cooking the beans in water at a simmer until they are soft, 45–60 minutes. Drain and set aside.

To make the asparagus crème: Melt the butter in a sauté pan. Add the garlic and shallot. Sauté until brown. Add the cream and asparagus. Simmer until the asparagus is soft. In a blender or food processor, puree the mixture. Season to taste with salt and pepper.

To make the brown butter vinaigrette: In a small pan over high heat, melt the butter and cook until it is brown and has a nutty aroma.

In a blender, combine the vinegar and honey. With the blender running, slowly drizzle in the brown butter and oil. Season to taste with salt and pepper.

To make the scallops: In a large frying pan over high heat, sear the scallops in the oil. Season to taste with salt and pepper. Add the potatoes to the pan, cut side down. Remove the scallops

from the pan and set aside. Keep warm. When the potatoes are cooked, add the cooked beans, ham, and tomatoes to heat through.

Dress the mâche with the vinaigrette. Chef Thorpe's note: Mâche can be found in most supermarkets, usually in the herb section.

To plate: Pour the asparagus crème on a serving plate. Spoon the potato mixture into the center of the plate. Place the scallops around the potato mixture. Top with the dressed mâche and serve immediately.

DeWolf Tavern

259 Thames Street
Bristol, RI 02809
(401) 254-2005
DEWOLFTAVERN.COM
Executive Chef Sai Viswanath

A genuine New England tavern and a chef from India trained in classical French cuisine—that is a most unusual recipe for success when it comes to Rhode Island restaurants. For the past decade, DeWolf Tavern in the seaside community of Bristol has been expanding its enthusiastic fan base, thanks to the chef and owner, Sai Viswanath.

If only the walls could talk at DeWolf Tavern, which dates back to 1818. In a way, they do talk. In the dining area on the upper level, sections of graffiti more than a century old can still be seen on a plastered wall. The building started out as a warehouse for the DeWolf brothers, who were rum producers. The lower level tavern is dark and moody with intimate booths and a fourteen-seat bar. The brighter upper level has a deck with a view of Bristol Harbor, the perfect spot for cocktails before dinner.

Viswanath is an interesting man. He holds degrees in culinary arts from a hotel school in Madras, India, and from the Culinary Institute of America. As a young man, he traveled the world, honing his skills at Indigo in Mumbai, considered one of the best restaurants in the world, and at the famed Union Square Cafe in New York City.

The chef's unique American-global menu at DeWolf Tavern reveals his respect for local seafood, as in the chorizo-crusted cod with roasted native corn, fenugreek, and tomato cream. His creative dishes combine local ingredients and flavors with the intensely high heat (900°F) of his charcoal-burning tandoor, a cylindrical clay oven used in cooking and baking throughout Asia. Roasted natural chicken, loin lamb chops, and spice-cured pork chops are all elevated to new heights after spending time in Viswanath's tandoor.

Viswanath's signature dish is his lobster popovers. The light and airy popovers are filled with lobster meat that has been sautéed in a light lobster-sherry sauce. The components of all his food are always interesting. Even side dishes are unusual—seasonal vegetables are served with toasted fresh coconut, the hash is made with brussels sprouts that are sautéed with corn bread and butter. His food is simply extraordinary.

KALE & ROMAINE SALAD WITH CORN BREAD

(SERVES 6)

For the corn bread:

Butter, for greasing the pan
Flour, for flouring the pan
¼ cup all-purpose flour
¾ cup cornmeal
1 tablespoon baking powder
½ teaspoon salt
2 large eggs
1 cup milk
6 tablespoons unsalted butter, melted
2 tablespoons honey

For the salad dressing:

1 lemon
Pinch of salt
¼ cup chopped parsley
¼ cup chopped tarragon
1 teaspoon minced garlic
1 cup mayonnaise
½ cup sour cream

For the salad:

1 head iceberg lettuce
2 heads heart of romaine
3 hard-boiled eggs, peeled
1 bunch kale, cleaned with stems removed
½ cup sunflower seeds

To make the corn bread: Preheat oven to 400°F.
Butter and flour a 9-inch square baking pan.

In a large bowl, whisk the flour with the cornmeal, baking powder, and salt. In a medium bowl, beat the eggs, then whisk in the milk, butter, and honey. Using a rubber spatula, lightly stir the wet ingredients into the dry. Stir just until blended. Scrape the batter into the prepared pan. Bake for about 25 minutes, or until the corn bread springs back when lightly pressed. Transfer the corn bread to a cooling rack. When cool, cut half the corn bread into ¾-inch cubes to make croutons. Wrap the remaining corn bread and reserve for another use.

To make the dressing: In a blender or food processor, combine the juice from a lemon, salt, parsley, tarragon, garlic, mayonnaise, and sour cream. Blend until combined.

To make the salad: Cut the head of iceberg lettuce into six large wedges. Cut off the bottoms of the romaine and peel off the leaves. Select three perfect romaine leaves for each plate. Place a wedge of iceberg lettuce on top of the romaine leaves.

Using a grater, shave just the white of the hard-boiled eggs over the lettuce leaves on each plate. Chop the kale and add to each plate. Sprinkle the sunflower seeds and olives over the top. Drizzle with dressing on top. Garnish with corn bread croutons.

CLAMS CHILI

(SERVES 6)

Olive oil, as needed

2 Spanish onions, cut into small dice

5 curry leaves

¼ cup thinly sliced garlic

½ teaspoon chile flakes

2 quarts canned crushed tomatoes

2 cups clam juice

48 littleneck clams, cleaned and soaked for 20 minutes

In a large sauté pan, heat just enough olive oil to coat the bottom of the pan. When the pan is hot, add the onions, curry leaves, and garlic. Sauté until translucent and soft. Be careful not to burn the garlic. Add the chile flakes and tomatoes. Cook for about 20 minutes. Add the clam juice to dilute. Add the clams in two batches (24 at a time).

Cook until the clams open. As each clam opens, remove it from the pan and place it in a large serving bowl. When all the clams are open and in the bowl, pour the sauce over the clams and serve immediately.

Chef Sai's note: If you are unable to find curry leaves at a specialty market, you can substitute thyme. This sauce goes very well with pasta.

Millonzi's Bar & Grille

11 Curson Street
West Warwick, RI 02893
(401) 615-7891
MILLONZISRI.COM
Executive Chef Kevin Millonzi

Kevin Millonzi is one of those chefs who paid his dues at wildly successful Providence restaurants such as the Atomic Grill and Prov, and now he owns and operates his own restaurant in the suburbs. At Millonzi's Bar & Grille in West Warwick, his innovative food is better than ever.

Since he graduated with highest honors from Johnson & Wales University's College of Culinary Arts, Millonzi has been wowing people with his delicious fusion cuisine, which continues at his namesake restaurant and through his well-respected catering division, Millonzi Fine Catering. The handsome young chef likes to say he serves "classic fare with a creative flair."

Take your basic fried calamari, for example. This particular dish is on almost every restaurant menu in Rhode Island, and it has even been nominated to be the state's official appetizer. But leave it to Chef Millonzi to take it to a new level. His calamari is dressed with a tomato-butter sauce with a hint of truffles and served with steamed littleneck clams, making it totally addictive.

His global dinner menu is filled with unusual dishes: Mozzarella Bon Bons, Shanghai Shrimp Bites, and Southwest Eggrolls, for appetizers. One of Millonzi's signature dishes, the house-made Tuscan Potato Chips, are drizzled with a Gorgonzola-scallion gravy. And yet all the basics are there to please everyone at the table, from grilled steak tips to baked haddock. Gluten-free items are also listed.

Millonzi's Bar & Grille is a small restaurant with sixty-five seats, including ten very comfortable spots at the bar. Booths and pub-height tables provide intimate dining for two as well as for small groups. The setting is dark and cozy, with a fireplace in the center of the dining area.

Truffle Calamari & Steamed Littleneck Clams

(SERVES 4)

For the calamari breading:

2 cups clam fry
1 cup all-purpose flour
1 teaspoon onion powder
1 teaspoon chile powder
½ teaspoon cayenne pepper
1 teaspoon sugar
1 teaspoon dried basil
Salt and pepper, to taste

For the compound butter:

8 ounces butter (2 sticks), at room temperature
1 tablespoon tomato paste
⅛ cup truffle oil
1 tablespoon chopped canned black
   truffle shavings
Salt and pepper, to taste

For the calamari and clams:

1 pound cleaned calamari, cut into rings
1 cup half and half
2 tablespoons olive oil
1 tablespoon chopped garlic
24 cleaned littleneck clams
2 cups dry white wine
1 cup chicken broth
1 tablespoon chopped fresh parsley

To make the calamari breading: In a large bowl, combine all the calamari breading ingredients. Mix well. Set aside.

To make the compound butter: Put the butter, tomato paste, truffle oil, and chopped truffles in the bowl of an electric stand mixer. Mix until ingredients are thoroughly combined. Season to taste with salt and pepper. Set aside.

To make the calamari and clams: In a large bowl, soak the calamari rings and tentacles in the half and half.

In a large skillet, combine the olive oil and garlic over high heat. Add the clams to the skillet, and sauté for 5 minutes. Deglaze the pan with wine and chicken broth. Add the compound butter mixture. Cover and simmer until the clams open.

Preheat a deep fryer (such as a Fry Daddy for home use) to 350°F, filled as recommended with oil. Dredge the calamari in the calamari breading. Submerge the calamari in batches in the fryer for 1 minute, or until crispy golden brown.

Toss the fried calamari in the skillet with the clams. Season to taste with salt and pepper.

Serve in a large bowl, family style. Sprinkle the chopped parsley over the clams just before serving.

Chef Millonzi's note: Garlic bread or Italian bread is a great item to serve on the side with this dish.

PERSIMMON

31 STATE STREET
BRISTOL, RI 02809
(401) 254-7474
PERSIMMONBRISTOL.COM
EXECUTIVE CHEF CHAMPE SPEIDEL

Any list of the top ten restaurants in Rhode Island would surely have Persimmon at the top, and most would agree that Executive Chef Champe Speidel creates the prettiest food imaginable.

In 2005, Champe and his wife, Lisa Speidel, opened Persimmon with just thirty-six seats (and four stools at an intimate bar). While he creates in the kitchen, she manages

the front of the house, warmly greeting appreciative customers. Persimmon is a modern, unassuming restaurant located in a quaint seaside town. Its simple olive-green exterior gives way to a cozy space with taupe walls, off-white trim, and touches of navy blue. On the walls are paintings of persimmons in shades of yellow-orange to dark red-orange by various artists.

Chef Speidel's food is just as colorful. Take the warm soup of Four Town Farm rainbow carrots and buttered lobster, for example. Served in a shallow soup bowl, the warm—not hot—soup is beyond delicious. The delicate garnish of sweet and tender lobster with glazed purple and golden carrots sits like a crown of jewels in the soup. Before you know it, you are scraping up every last drop with your soup spoon and this precious soup is gone.

Or consider the pan-roasted lamb loin with parsnip puree. The perfectly trimmed loins are seared and flavored with garlic and rosemary. Chef Speidel knows his meats— he was a butcher before he became a chef. When he isn't in the Persimmon kitchen, he can be found at his butcher shop in Barrington. Persimmon Provisions is an immaculate butchery with refrigerated cases of everything from duck to artisanal cheeses. The small shop funnels the very best products to the Persimmon kitchen, where Chef Speidel and his well-trained crew turn out dishes that are truly works of art splashed with bright colors.

The American cuisine served at Persimmon is rooted in the impeccable ingredients that Chef Speidel demands, and in techniques far beyond the average cook. In his own words, the chef is fiercely committed to sourcing the very best ingredients from near and far. The menu changes slightly every night to keep things interesting for regular guests. The result is a one-of-a-kind creative dining experience.

WARM SOUP OF FOUR TOWN FARM RAINBOW CARROTS & BUTTERED LOBSTER

(SERVES 4)

Chef Speidel's note: This dish utilizes all possible uses of the incredible carrots we get from our favorite farm. We glaze the carrots in their own juice, add a touch of cream, and then puree them in a blender. Next we try to make the dish interesting by adding carrots cooked by different methods—glazed, slow-roasted, dehydrated, and raw—to add some texture and depth. For a touch of luxury, we add gently cooked lobster, which goes beautifully with carrots. Finally we add a hint of caraway, fennel, and dill as they are all part of the same botanical family, Umbelliferae. All this is very simple indeed and should not take more than an hour from start to finish. Also, use caution when adding too many purple or red carrots as they will bleed into the others, creating a very unpleasant brown color.

For the soup:

2 cups assorted carrots, such as Chantenay, orange round, red dragon, pink, yellow, and purple
1 cup carrot juice, from about 2–3 orange carrots
Salt, as desired
Pinch of sugar
2 cups water
1 teaspoon toasted caraway seeds
½ cup cream

For the glazed carrots:

4–5 assorted petite carrots (no longer than 4 inches), peeled, cut into obliques, with tops removed
1 teaspoon sugar
2 teaspoons salt
½ cup water
2 fresh dill sprigs
1 tablespoon unsalted butter

For the lobster:

1 teaspoon water
2 tablespoons unsalted butter
Meat from a cooked 1-pound lobster, cut into 1-inch pieces
1 teaspoon salt

½ teaspoon fennel pollen or ground fennel seed
1 teaspoon minced parsley

For the optional garnish:

Green carrot tops, rinsed and dried in a salad spinner
Wild carrot flowers
Raw carrots shaved very thin
Sprinkle of caraway seed powder

To make the soup: In a heavy pot large enough to hold all the carrots in one layer, combine the carrots, carrot juice, salt, and sugar, and bring to a boil. Skim any froth or scum off the surface of the liquid, and allow it to reduce down to a glaze. This may take 5–7 minutes, but every stove is different. Check the pot often to ensure it does not burn. Once the juice boils down to a glaze, stir the carrots to coat evenly and then add the water. Bring the liquid back to a boil, then turn down to a simmer for another 10–15 minutes.

In another small pot, toast the caraway seeds until fragrant, then add the cream and bring to a boil. Once the cream comes to a boil, remove from the heat and cover with plastic wrap or a lid to infuse for at least 15 minutes. After the infusion,

add the entire mix to the simmering carrot soup and bring back to a boil.

Start tasting the soup for proper seasoning. It's easier to fix the seasoning now rather than after pureeing.

The soup is now ready to puree. Strain the soup through a large sieve or colander, saving the liquid. In a large blender, add the solids, in batches if necessary, and blend on high for at least 1 full minute per batch. Add enough of the strained liquid to help the blender blades turn and create a vortex. Strain the blended mixture through a very fine sieve, using the back of a ladle if necessary to push the soup through. If the soup is too thick, add more cooking liquid to achieve the desired consistency. If using right away, keep warm with a lid on top. Otherwise the soup base can be cooled and stored in the refrigerator for another 2 days.

To make the glazed carrots: In a heavy-bottomed saucepan, place all the glazed carrot ingredients in a single layer. The water should cover the carrots by 1 inch; if not, add more water. Bring to a boil, then reduce the heat to a simmer. Cook the carrots until all the water has evaporated, about 10 minutes. The carrots should be tender and the butter and sugar should have effectively glazed them. Discard the dill sprigs and keep the carrots warm while you prepare the lobster.

To make the lobster: In a small pot, combine the water and butter, and bring to a boil. Using a small wire whisk, stir until the butter melts. Add the lobster, salt, and fennel pollen (or seed). Cook just until the lobster is warm; take care not to overcook. Remove from the heat and keep warm. This should be done just before you are ready to serve the soup.

To serve: Warm four wide soup bowls in a low oven for 1 minute. Arrange the glazed carrots and lobster attractively in the warm bowls, either in the center or around the perimeter. Bring the soup base back to a boil. Froth with an immersion blender or a wire whisk to blend and aerate the soup.

Pour the soup into the bowls at the table in front of your guests. Garnish each bowl with a little of the minced parsley. Garnish with more flair using some green carrot tops, rinsed and dried in a salad spinner, wild carrot flowers, raw carrots shaved very thin, and a sprinkle of caraway seed powder.

Pan-Roasted Lamb Loin
with Parsnip Puree & Light Pan Sauce
(SERVES 4)

For the lamb loin:

1–2 tablespoons canola oil

2 boneless lamb loins (also called cannons),
 with fat trimmed

Salt and freshly cracked black pepper, to taste

3 tablespoons unsalted butter, divided

1 tablespoon minced shallot

1 tablespoon minced garlic

½ cup lamb or beef stock (if neither is available,
 chicken stock is also fine)

1 tablespoon minced chives

1 tablespoon minced rosemary

For the parsnip puree:

¾ pound parsnips, peeled and cut into even
 1-inch pieces

1 cup milk

1 cup heavy cream

1 teaspoon sugar

1 tablespoon salt

To make the lamb: Heat a large skillet with a tablespoon of oil until it begins to smoke. Season the lamb loins with salt and place into the skillet very carefully. You should hear a nice sizzle; if not, then your pan is not hot enough. Sear the lamb loins on each side until you achieve a golden brown color, basting the lamb from time to time with the oil. Cook to your desired doneness, then remove the lamb from the skillet and allow it to rest on a plate. Season the lamb with another sprinkle of salt and pepper.

In the same skillet that held the lamb, pour off any remaining oil and add a pat of butter. When the butter has melted, add the shallots and garlic, taking care not to brown them. Add the stock and any juices that have come from the resting lamb, and reduce the mixture in the pan by half. Now add the herbs and whisk in the remaining butter. Taste the sauce for proper seasoning, and strain through a fine-mesh sieve into a warm sauce vessel or gravy boat.

To make the parsnip puree: Place all the parsnip ingredients in a large enough saucepot and bring to a simmer over medium heat. Cook until the parsnips are tender when pierced with the tip of a knife. Strain the parsnips, saving the liquid, and then place them into a blender. Pulse the blender to break up the parsnips, adding enough liquid to allow the mixture to blend smoothly. Strain the puree through a fine sieve using a ladle or rubber spatula to work the mixture through the mesh. Keep warm and covered if using right away, or place in the refrigerator for up to 2 days.

To serve: Cut each lamb loin into four pieces and place two pieces of lamb on each of the four warm dinner plates. Spoon a dollop of parsnip puree on the plate. Spoon some sauce over the lamb and serve immediately.

POTENZA RISTORANTE-BAR

162 MAYFIELD AVENUE
CRANSTON, RI 02920
(401) 273-2652
POTENZARISTORANTE.COM
EXECUTIVE CHEF WALTER POTENZA

There's something special about a restaurant that's located in a house, a home once occupied by a family that sat around the dining room table on a regular basis to talk about the day and to share good food. That's what awaits you at Potenza Ristorante-Bar in a residential section of Cranston.

This is the latest venture from Walter Potenza and Carmela Natale. Walter is the executive chef and Carmela is at the front of the house greeting guests for dinner. Their Cape Cod–style house has been reconfigured with intimate dining areas and a small bar. This duo is well known throughout Rhode Island for their past restaurants, and Walter is considered the godfather of Italian cuisine by many. When he isn't cooking in his restaurant kitchen, he offers cooking classes. Walter simply has too many awards and honors to mention. He is committed to authentic Italian regional cooking and hospitality. Walter is an expert on Italian-Jewish foods as well as gluten-free cooking and clay cookery. His various menus reflect his constant search for fresh, sustainable, and local ingredients.

Every month a different region of Italy is explored in special prix-fixe dinners. Dishes on the nightly dinner menu are listed in Italian with English translations. Typical offerings include *pennette carbonara* (traditional Abruzzese quill-shaped pasta with crispy

pancetta, peas, egg yolk, black pepper, and aged Pecorino Romano blended with a light vegetable broth) and *gabbia di pollo* (all-natural chicken tenderloins with porcini mushrooms, sweet Gorgonzola, veal demi-glacé, a touch of cream, and Pinot Grigio over risotto). Some of his gluten-free specialties are a lentil-salmon roll and gnocchi made from chickpea flour with a brilliant green pea pesto. For a gluten-free dessert, the master chef likes to serve *castagnole,* sugar-dusted chickpea fritters that are irresistible.

CHICKPEA FLOUR GNOCCHI WITH PEA PESTO
(SERVES 6)

For the pea pesto:

4 tablespoons extra-virgin olive oil, divided

3 garlic cloves, sliced

1½ cups dry peas

Pinch of salt

2 cups fresh spinach

¼ cup walnuts, toasted

Kosher salt and white pepper, to taste

For the gnocchi:

2¼ pounds potatoes (Idaho varietals preferred)

1 cup chickpea flour

1 egg

⅛ teaspoon freshly grated nutmeg

2 tablespoons Parmigiano-Reggiano or Grana
    Padano cheese

Kosher salt, to taste

To make the pea pesto: In a medium-size saucepan, heat 1 tablespoon of olive oil. Cook the garlic in the oil for 30 seconds. Add the dry peas, mix well, and cover with 4 cups of water and a pinch of salt. Cook the peas until soft, about 35 minutes. Add the spinach and cook for another 5 minutes. Remove from the heat and set aside. Add the walnuts, remaining olive oil, salt, and white pepper to the pea-spinach mixture. Puree in a food processor until smooth. Set aside.

To make the gnocchi: Boil the potatoes in salted water until tender, about 20 minutes; drain and peel. Pass the potatoes through a fine disk of a potato ricer; allow to cool. Pour onto a counter.

Sift the flour over the potatoes. Work in the egg, nutmeg, and grated cheese until a dough forms. Knead well for 8 minutes. Cut the dough into 6 pieces; roll into finger-thick logs. Cut each log into ½-inch pieces. As the gnocchi are ready, place them on a floured tray.

Bring a pot of water to a boil. Add the gnocchi and salt. With a slotted spoon, move the gnocchi to a bowl as they rise to the surface. Reserve 1 cup of the cooking water to dilute the sauce. Pour pea pesto over the cooked gnocchi, mix well, and serve hot.

Chef Walter's note: Pea pesto may be kept in the refrigerator for several days, and its color will not alter if totally covered with vegetable oil on the surface. It also can be used as a flavor enhancer for soups, or as a topping for your favorite crostini and bruschetta. If too thick, dilute with vegetable stock or water.

LENTIL-SALMON ROLL
(SERVES 6)

½ cup chopped onions

1 bay leaf

¾ cup dry brown lentils, soaked for 2 hours, drained

3 tablespoons extra-virgin olive oil, divided, plus extra

4 scallions, sliced, divided

1 pound clams, scrubbed

1 thyme sprig

2 tablespoons fresh minced parsley, plus extra
    for garnish

Kosher salt and freshly ground black pepper, to taste

2 pounds boneless salmon in 1 piece, skin removed

Sesame seeds, as needed for coating

1 garlic clove, minced

1 rosemary sprig

Bring a pot of water to a boil. Add the onions, bay leaf, and lentils, and cook for 40 minutes. Meanwhile, in a skillet over medium heat, warm 1 tablespoon of olive oil. Add three scallions and sauté for 5 minutes. Set aside.

In a saucepan over medium heat, combine the clams with the thyme and the remaining scallion and cook until the clams open, about 5 minutes. Remove the clam meat from their shells and set aside. Strain the cooking liquid and set it aside.

Preheat the oven to 325°F.

Drain the lentils, discard the bay leaf, and transfer half of the lentils to a food processor. Add the parsley and the sautéed scallion. Season with salt and pepper. Puree until smooth.

Butterfly the salmon fillet: Slice it halfway through the middle of the fillet and across toward either side. Open the salmon fillet like a book to form a larger, thinner rectangle of fish. Trim the fillet, and add the trimmings to the food processor, and pulse again.

Spread the salmon-lentil puree onto the surface of the fillet, and roll it up. Coat the outside with sesame seeds and wrap the stuffed salmon roll in a sheet of parchment paper. Tie with butcher's twine to close, and place in a baking dish. Rub the parchment paper with olive oil, and bake in the preheated 325°F oven for 20 minutes.

Meanwhile, in a skillet over medium heat, warm the remaining olive oil. Add the garlic, rosemary, and remaining lentils, and sauté. Deglaze with the reserved clam juice, and cook until it evaporates. Remove and discard the garlic and rosemary, and transfer half of the sauce to a food processor. Pulse several times until a smooth consistency is achieved. Unwrap the salmon roll, and slice into portions.

To serve, spread the pureed sauce on a platter, and arrange the salmon pieces on top. Scatter the reserved clams and lentils around, and garnish with parsley.

CASTAGNOLE

(SERVES 10)

Chef Walter's note: These fritters are traditionally served to children at Carnevale (an Italian holiday similar to Mardi Gras) and earned their names because of their chestnut shapes. *Castagna* is the Italian word for chestnut.

4¾ cups gluten-free flour (available in specialty markets)
1 cup chestnut flour (available in specialty markets)
1¼ cups sugar
¼ teaspoon salt
1 teaspoon baking powder
6 eggs, beaten
1 cup whole milk
1 tablespoon rum
1 teaspoon vanilla extract
3⅓ cups extra-virgin olive oil, divided
Grated zest of 1 lemon
1 tablespoon anise seeds
Confectioners' sugar, as needed

Combine the flours, sugar, salt, and baking powder in a bowl. Make a well in the center. Add the eggs, milk, rum, vanilla extract, ⅓ cup of the olive oil, lemon zest, and anise seeds. Stir the ingredients together until they form a mass, adding a little water or milk if necessary to make a soft, smooth dough.

In a deep pot, heat the remaining olive oil until it registers 325°F on a thermometer. Drop in spoonfuls of the dough, a few at a time, and fry until they are puffy and golden on both sides, about 3 minutes. Remove with a slotted spoon and blot dry on paper towels. When you have fried all the *castagnole,* dust them with confectioners' sugar, and serve hot.

RASOI

727 EAST AVENUE
PAWTUCKET, RI 02860
(401) 728-5500
INDIANRESTAURANTSRI.COM
OWNER–EXECUTIVE CHEF SANJIV DHAR

Quite possibly the most colorful restaurant in Rhode Island, Rasoi is not just another Indian eatery. Located in a strip mall dotted with ethnic restaurants, Rasoi stands out with its vibrant yellow, red, and blue color scheme and vivid scenes from India hanging on the walls. At the heart of this neighborhood restaurant is a four-sided bar, where individuals dining alone will feel most welcome.

Owner–Executive Chef Sanjiv Dhar and his team have created a restaurant that offers healthy Indian food and attentive service. The menu is both traditional and creative, featuring the diverse regions of India. Vegan choices are available as well as gluten-free and dairy-free dishes. All-you-can-eat lunch buffets are offered every Saturday and Sunday.

From southern India comes Chicken Varuval, an appetizer cooked on a tawa griddle. The all-time New Delhi favorite is the Chicken Tikka Labradar, cubes of chicken marinated in yogurt, ginger, and garlic, grilled, and then cooked in tomato sauce. Goan fish curry cooked with coconut milk and tamarind is a dish from India's coastal area. Other regional dishes include Shrimp and Scallops Moilee from Kerala on the coast. The Punjabi-style Lamb Saag consists of chunks of lamb loin cooked in a spinach puree.

The chef-owner is a remarkable man. He makes regular trips back to his homeland of India, and he shares his knowledge of Indian cuisine with those who sign up for his cooking classes. His award-winning 85-seat restaurant was designed to give all diners an unobstructed view of the open kitchen. Rasoi is the Hindi word for kitchen.

(The exotic ingredients in Dhar's recipes can be found in ethnic specialty markets, such as Not Just Spices at 836 Hope Street in Providence.)

Dhar also owns two other Indian restaurants in Rhode Island. Kabob and Curry is located at 261 Thayer Street in Providence, and Rasa is at 149 Main Street in East Greenwich.

SHRIMP MOILEE

(SERVES 4)

1 pound shrimp, shelled and deveined,
   with tails left on
1 teaspoon salt
2 teaspoons freshly squeezed lemon juice
1 tablespoon vegetable oil
1 teaspoon mustard seeds
8–10 fresh curry leaves
2 medium onions, chopped
2 teaspoons fresh ginger paste
2 teaspoons fresh garlic paste
3 green chiles, stemmed and slit open
1 teaspoon ground turmeric
1½ cups coconut milk

Place the shrimp in a large bowl. Sprinkle with salt and lemon juice. Set aside for 15 minutes.

Place a nonstick pan over medium heat. Add the oil to the pan. Add the mustard seeds. As soon as they start to sizzle, add the curry leaves and onions. Cook until the onions are translucent.

Add the ginger and garlic pastes and green chiles. Sauté for another minute. Add the turmeric and shrimp. Stir to coat the shrimp with all the herbs and spices. Cook over high heat for 30 seconds, stirring constantly.

Add the coconut milk. Simmer for 5 minutes or until the shrimp are cooked. Adjust the seasonings before serving.

KERALA CHICKEN STEW

(SERVES 4)

5 tablespoons olive oil

1½ teaspoons whole black peppercorns

3 cinnamon sticks

10 cloves

8 green cardamom pods

3 medium onions, cut in half lengthwise and then cut into half rings

1-inch piece of ginger, peeled, sliced, and cut into fine slivers

6 green chiles, slit open

3 pounds chicken, skinned and cut into small pieces

2 tablespoons coriander powder

1 teaspoon turmeric powder

1 quart water

3 medium all-purpose potatoes, peeled and cut lengthwise into 1-inch thick pieces

Salt, as needed

2½ cups coconut milk

1 tablespoon lemon juice

Oil, as needed

4 tablespoons finely sliced shallots

15 fresh kaffir lime leaves

In a large pot, heat the oil over medium heat. Add the peppercorns, cinnamon sticks, cloves, and cardamom. Stir once. Add the onions and ginger. Sauté until the onions are translucent. Add the green chiles and chicken pieces. Brown the chicken for 2–3 minutes. Add the coriander powder and turmeric powder. Mix well. Add the water and bring to a boil. Cover with a lid. Simmer on low for about 10 minutes.

Add the potatoes and salt. Stir. Bring to a boil. Cover and cook on low heat for another 15–20 minutes until the chicken and potatoes are tender. Add the coconut milk and lemon juice. Cook for 3 minutes on low heat.

In a small pan, heat a little oil. Add the sliced shallots. Stir until they are lightly browned. Add the kaffir lime leaves. Stir. Pour this mixture into the chicken stew. Serve immediately.

Simone's

275 Child Street
Warren, RI 02885
(401) 247-1200
simonesri.com
Executive Chef Joe Simone

Joe Simone is a chef's chef. Many of the hot new chefs on the Rhode Island restaurant scene are fans of this unpretentious man who simply loves to cook good food. For years he was the smiling face in the semi-open kitchen at The Sunnyside in Warren, and he would always give a friendly wave to friends and regular customers. In late 2012, they were stunned when Joe announced he was closing that beloved restaurant, but the good news is that Joe Simone has opened a new namesake restaurant.

Simone's opened in early 2014, and it was one of those much-anticipated openings. With eighty-two seats inside and another twenty-five outdoors, the new Simone's is almost twice as big as The Sunnyside, and it did not disappoint its many fans. Joe is back in the kitchen with most of his former crew, including his brother John, one of the best bartenders around.

The even bigger news is that Simone's will be serving dinner. The Sunnyside was named for its sunny dining room that served only breakfast, lunch, and brunch, a concept Joe called Daytime Dining. The new Simone's continues its award-winning tradition of daytime dining, plus it now offers a nighttime menu.

No matter what time of day it is, Joe calls himself a Mediterranean cook because he has spent a great deal of time in that part of the world. You'll also always find a few Mexican dishes on the menu from Joe's years in California. His culinary focus continues to be on pure, clean, and traditional flavors, evident in his line of jams and spice rubs for sale at the restaurant, and he teaches that philosophy to folks who sign up for his cooking classes.

Simone's is committed to being involved with the local community, and Chef Simone continues to support local farmers, producers, and vendors. What else would you expect from a chef who signs off with "Peace, Love, and Deliciousness."

GRILLED CLAMS WITH DILL OREGANATO

(SERVES 4–8)

24 fresh littleneck clams, washed in cool water
    to remove all sand

½ cup extra-virgin olive oil

2 tablespoons chopped fresh dill

1 tablespoon chopped Italian parsley

1 tablespoon minced garlic

Grated zest of 2 lemons

½ teaspoon kosher salt, more or less to taste

½ teaspoon crushed red chile peppers,
    more or less to taste

Chef Simone's note: You can make the herb and garlic dressing (oreganato) a few days in advance. Cover and refrigerate it until an hour or two before grilling the clams.

In a nonreactive bowl, combine all the ingredients except the clams.

Preheat your grill. When the grill is hot, place the washed and dried clams on the grill and cook for about 8 minutes, turning each clam over once or twice, until the clams open. As each clam opens, move it to a serving bowl and spoon a tiny bit of the oreganato on top of the meat inside each clam. When all the grilled clams are in the bowl, serve immediately.

Halibut Roast with Spinach & Mushroom Gratin

(SERVES 4–6)

For the spinach & mushroom gratin:

1 pound spinach
1 pound cremini or other mushrooms, sliced
1 tablespoon olive oil
Salt, to taste
1 cup milk
2 tablespoons unsalted butter
2 tablespoons flour

For the halibut:

2 pounds halibut fillets (or other firm, flaky white fish like cod), cut into serving-size portions
Salt, to taste
2 cups panko bread crumbs, unseasoned preferred
1 tablespoon fresh lemon juice, more or less to taste
2 tablespoons olive oil
1 heaping teaspoon dried herbes de Provence or oregano, thyme, or whatever spices/herbs you like

Chef Simone's note: You may prepare the spinach and mushroom gratin up to two days in advance. Simply store the mixture covered in the refrigerator.

To make the spinach and mushroom gratin: Wash the spinach in cool water and remove the stems. Blanch the spinach in boiling salted water. When tender, in 1 minute or so, carefully drain it. Spread the cooked spinach out to cool on a cookie sheet lined with a double layer of paper towels. When it's cool enough to handle, gather up the spinach to form balls that you can squeeze over the sink to extract as much water as possible. Coarsely chop the blanched and dried spinach.

In a saucepan, combine the mushrooms and olive oil. Season with salt. Cover and cook for 30 minutes, stirring occasionally, until the mushrooms have given up their liquid. Remove from the heat and set aside.

In a saucepan, heat the milk until it almost simmers. Set the milk aside while you begin the roux.

In a large saucepan over medium heat, melt the butter. When it starts to sizzle, add the flour and whisk for 1 minute until you can detect a nutty aroma. Slowly whisk in the hot milk. Lower the heat and cook, stirring constantly while the mixture thickens. Add the cooked mushrooms and their juices. Continue stirring until the mixture thickens once again, in about 2 minutes, depending on how hot the mushrooms are when you add them. (This is called a béchamel.)

To finish the gratin, fold the chopped spinach into the mushroom béchamel. It should have a slightly dry texture. Taste and add more salt, if needed.

To make the halibut: Preheat oven to 400°F.

Spray a large baking dish with Pam. Spoon the spinach and mushroom gratin mixture over the bottom of the pan. You should have about ½ inch of the gratin mixture in the pan.

Season each piece of halibut with salt, and arrange "nice side up" on top of the gratin.

In a small bowl, toss the panko with the lemon juice, olive oil, and herbs. Sprinkle the crumb mixture over the fish and gratin. Bake for 12–15 minutes, or until the fish is just cooked through and the crumbs are golden brown and crispy.

BUTTERSCOTCH PUDDING

(SERVES 8)

1 cup dark brown sugar

4 tablespoons cornstarch

Generous pinch of salt

4 cups heavy cream

4 tablespoons unsalted butter

1 tablespoon vanilla extract, more or less to taste

Whipped cream, as needed (optional)

Chef Simone's note: I like to use a silicone whisk when I make this recipe, which can be made up to 3 days in advance.

In a medium-size saucepan, combine the dark brown sugar, cornstarch, and salt using a whisk. Continue whisking as you add the cream. Set the pan over medium heat and slowly it bring to a simmer, whisking often, scraping around the edges with a high-temperature rubber spatula.

When the mixture approaches a simmer, whisk constantly until thickened. Make sure you scrape the sides of the pan to prevent lumps.

When the pudding has thickened, remove the pan from the heat. Whisk in the butter and vanilla. Transfer the pudding to one large bowl or eight custard cups. Refrigerate for up to 3 days. Serve cold with whipped cream, if desired.

Twin Oaks

100 Sabra Street
Cranston, RI 02910
(401) 781-9693
TWINOAKSREST.COM
Executive Chef Bill Smith

Many Rhode Islanders went to Twin Oaks when they were kids for family dinners, and now they go there with their children and even their grandchildren. This suburban restaurant has been around since the 1920s, when it operated as a basement speakeasy

with its own still. Federal agents destroyed the still in 1933, and that led owner William DeAngelus to open a restaurant called Twin Oaks on that site. The DeAngelus family still owns the business, with Chef Bill Smith in charge of the busy kitchen.

This is a huge, old-school restaurant often described as "a poor man's country club." That is, you won't find cutting-edge dishes on the menu. Instead, expect Italian classics such as veal parmesan and traditional New England fare like Yankee pot roast. The menu is almost as big as the restaurant, which seats 650 plus another 42 on the deck overlooking Spectacle Lake. Twin Oaks is also known for its generous servings, whether it's the twenty-ounce Black Angus sirloin steak or any of the oversized cocktails served by friendly bartenders. Many staff members have been there for decades.

Named for the oak trees that grace the waterfront property, Twin Oaks has regular daily specials suggested by the chef: meat loaf every Tuesday, chicken pesto penne on Wednesday, and tenderloin tips on Thursday. Fish delicacies, including their famous baked stuffed shrimp, are popular on Friday while beef is the weekend specialty. The secret recipe Twin Oaks pasta sauce is bottled and sold on the premises.

Grub Street, a blog about the restaurant scene in American cities, posted "50 State Dinners: Food Treks Worth Taking" to spotlight some of the best food in America. When it came to Rhode Island, they chose Twin Oaks. They wrote: "This is the type of place your parents took you when you were a kid. That means Yankee fare Grandma would approve of (liver and onions, baked scrod) and of course that Rhode Island specialty, quahog pie. There are surely fancier restaurants in the Providence area, and certainly more innovative ones. But for sheer atmosphere and nostalgia, you just can't beat Twin Oaks."

BAKED STUFFED SHRIMP

(SERVES 16–20)

5 pounds jumbo shrimp
2 pounds butter
1 garlic clove, chopped
2 tablespoons chopped parsley
1¾ pounds buttery crackers, ground
1 cup fine bread crumbs

Preheat the oven to 400°F.

Peel the shrimp, split its underside, and remove the black vein. Place the shrimp on an ungreased baking sheet. Set aside.

Melt the butter over medium-high heat. Add the garlic and sauté for 5 minutes or until softened. Remove the garlic from the pan before it browns. Add the parsley, cracker crumbs, and bread crumbs. Mix until blended.

Spoon the buttery mixture into the cavity on each shrimp. Bake at 400°F for 15 minutes.

STUFFED FILLET OF SOLE FLORENTINE

(SERVES 6)

1 garlic clove

1 cup olive oil

1 pound cooked spinach

6 ounces grated cheddar cheese

30 black olives, sliced

4 tablespoons butter, melted

4 tablespoons lemon juice

18 Ritz crackers, crushed

1 cup bread crumbs

18 (3-ounce) sole fillets

Salt and red pepper flakes, to taste

18 slices mozzarella cheese, each slice 1 inch wide

In a saucepan, lightly brown the garlic in the oil. Remove the garlic from the pan. Add the spinach to the oil for added flavor. As soon as the spinach wilts, remove it from the pan. Place the spinach in a mixing bowl. Add the grated cheddar cheese and olives. Mix thoroughly.

Preheat oven to 425°F.

In a small bowl, combine the melted butter and lemon juice. Mix well. In another bowl, combine the crushed crackers and bread crumbs.

On a large cutting board, lay out the sole fillets. Season with salt and red pepper flakes. Place one slice of mozzarella on each fillet. Add a heaping tablespoon of the spinach mixture. Roll up the fillets and place them in an oiled baking pan. Brush with the mixture of melted butter and lemon juice. Sprinkle with a mixture of crushed crackers and bread crumbs. Bake in the preheated oven for 20 minutes.

2 Pauls' City Grille

315 Waterman Avenue
East Providence, RI 02914
(401) 228-Paul
2paulsgoodfood.com
Executive Chef Paul Shire

Paul Shire is a chef with a devoted fan base that has been following him for more than twenty years as he moved from one hot restaurant to another in the Providence area. Now he co-owns 2 Pauls' City Grille with his business partner, Paul Roidoulis. They met on the golf course and discovered a shared love of music and good food.

"We became fast friends and always wanted to team up to create a great place to eat," said Shire. "A place where you feel wanted, without any pretentious attitude or tiny portions. Just good food and plenty of it."

Together they created the 2 Pauls concept, a neighborhood restaurant serving casual comfort food.

One dish that Shire's fans crave is his famous meat loaf, made with rolled oats. It's a recipe that he has prepared throughout his culinary career. At 2 Pauls' City Grille, the home-style meat loaf is served true to form—generous slices of the twice-cooked meat loaf accompanied by garlic mashed potatoes, bourbon whiskey gravy, and crispy fried onions. Another favorite dish is Shire's calamari with local squid fried just until tender and then tossed in garlic-herb butter and mixed hot peppers.

Shire's menu is eclectic, from down-home chicken potpie to Chianti-braised beef short ribs. The seasonal menu is also global—Shrimp Mozambique, Prince Edward Island mussels, Maryland crab cakes, Jamaican jerk chicken, and American chop suey. Creative menu items include polenta fries served with melted Gorgonzola cheese and eggplant patties topped with a zippy marinara sauce.

Cooking is definitely in Shire's blood. His great grandfather was the chef to the king of Egypt. His aunt is Lydia Shire, the famous Boston restaurateur.

TWICE-COOKED MEAT LOAF

(SERVES 12)

5 pounds ground beef
3 whole eggs
2 onions, chopped
1¾ cups tomato juice
2½ cups rolled quick oats
Salt and pepper, to taste
Worcestershire sauce, to taste
Water, as needed

In a large bowl, combine the ground beef with the eggs, chopped onions, tomato juice, and oats. Mix evenly by hand. Season to taste with salt, pepper, and Worcestershire sauce. Continue to work the meat mixture by hand until smooth.

Preheat oven to 325°F.

Place the meat mixture on a large sheet pan. Shape into an oblong loaf. Use the palm of your hand to slap out any air and cracks that form in each loaf. Wet each loaf with a little water, and rub the loaves smooth. Drizzle more water onto the sheet pan to prevent the loaves from drying or cracking.

Bake in the preheated 325°F oven (a convection oven is recommended). After 45 minutes, increase the oven temperature to 350°F. Bake for another 45 minutes, or until an internal temperature of about 165°F is reached.

When done, remove the loaf from the oven. Place the loaf on a rack in the refrigerator. Cool the loaf completely.

To serve, cut the loaf into equal size slices. In a nonstick frying pan, sauté each slice until heated through. Serve with your favorite brown gravy recipe. (Chef Paul Shire makes his meat loaf gravy with a bit of bourbon whiskey.)

EGGPLANT PATTIES WITH MARINARA SAUCE

(SERVES 6)

1 large eggplant, peeled and diced

2 cups grated Romano cheese

1 small onion, finely diced

2 eggs

4 tablespoons coarsely chopped Italian parsley

4 cups coarse white bread crumbs (stale Italian bread or panko work well)

Salt, pepper, and red pepper flakes, to taste

Flour, as needed

Oil, as needed for frying

Marinara sauce

Additional grated cheese

Blanch the eggplant in lightly salted water for 3–5 minutes, or until soft. Place the blanched eggplant in a strainer set over a large bowl. Place in the refrigerator to drain and cool.

Once cool, press out the remaining water by hand squeezing the eggplant. Place the eggplant in a large bowl with the grated cheese, diced onion, eggs, parsley, bread crumbs, salt, pepper, and red pepper flakes. Mix well. Form into 12 patties.

Dust the patties with flour before frying them in a little oil in a large skillet. Fry the patties until golden brown on both sides. Serve with your favorite marinara sauce and grated cheese. Allow two patties per person.

Index

About the Author

Linda Beaulieu is the author of nine books, all dealing with food and restaurants, including the definitive *Providence and Rhode Island Cookbook,* now in its second edition. During the past thirty years, Linda has written for local, regional, and national publications, winning numerous awards along the way. She is a James Beard Award winner for an article she wrote on Native American food for the *National Culinary Review.* A graduate of Northeastern University in Boston, Linda has also worked in public relations, specializing in restaurants and chefs. She is married to Brian Beaulieu, a now-retired journalist, and they are the human parents of an incredibly smart cocker spaniel named Beau. The Beaulieu family resides in Lincoln, Rhode Island, and they have a summer home in Narragansett.

About the Photographer

Al Weems is a corporate, commercial, and advertising photographer specializing in on-location assignments. His educational background includes a bachelor's degree in psychology and business as well. He has photographed throughout the United States and internationally, and he has conducted many workshops and seminars. He is Rhode Island–based living in Sutton, Mass. Al has been published in numerous magazines, annual reports, and catalogs. He is a "natural light" photographer, preferring that method over the use of artificial lighting sources.